WARRANT FOR TERROR

Fatwās of Radical Islam and the Duty of Jihād

SHMUEL BAR

HOOVER STUDIES
IN POLITICS, ECONOMICS,
AND SOCIETY

Published in cooperation with
HOOVER INSTITUTION
Stanford University • Stanford, California

ROWMAN & LITTLEFIELD PUBLISHERS, INC.
Lanham • Boulder • New York • Toronto • Oxford

ROWMAN & LITTLEFIELD PUBLISHERS, INC.

The Hoover Institution on War, Revolution and Peace, founded at Stanford University in 1919 by Herbert Hoover, who went on to become the thirty-first president of the United States, is an interdisciplinary research center for advanced study on domestic and international affairs. The views expressed in its publications are entirely those of the authors and do not necessarily reflect the views of the staff, officers, or Board of Overseers of the Hoover Institution.

www.hoover.org

Published in the United States of America
by Rowman & Littlefield Publishers, Inc.
A wholly owned subsidary of The Rowman & Littlefield Publishing Group, Inc.
4501 Forbes Boulevard, Suite 200, Lanham, Maryland 20706
www.rowmanlittlefield.com
PO Box 317
Oxford
OX2 9RU, UK
Distributed by National Book Network

Copyright © 2006 by the Board of Trustees of the
Leland Stanford Junior University
Published in cooperation with the Hoover Institution at Stanford University.
First paperback edition 2008

British Library Cataloguing in Publication Information Available

Library of Congress Cataloging-in-Publication Data
Bar, Shmuel.
Warrant for terror : fatwas of radical Islam and the duty of jihad /
Shmuel Bar.
    p.   cm.—(Hoover studies in politics, economics, and society)
"Published in cooperation with Hoover Institution."
Includes bibliographical references and index.
1. Terrorism—Religious aspects—Islam.   2. Jihad.   3. Fatwas.
I. Title.   II. Series.
HV6431.B353 2006
363.325'1—dc22   2006001837

ISBN-13: 978–0-7425–5120–6 (cloth : alk. paper)
ISBN-10: 0–7425–5120–2 (cloth : alk. paper)
ISBN-13: 978–0-7425–5121–3 (pbk. : alk. paper)
ISBN-10: 0–7425–5121–0 (pbk. : alk. paper)

Contents

Preface

THIS BOOK—the result of a long-standing interest in the use of Islamic religious arguments to justify acts of violence and terrorism—is based on a large corpus of documents collected over many years. The main findings arising from these documents were first published in *Policy Review* 125 (June–July 2004). Reactions to that article showed a growing public interest. That, along with the need to elaborate on some of the issues, led me to return to the topic.

I am grateful to the Hoover Institution and particularly to Peter Berkowitz and to Tod Lindberg for encouraging me to write this book and for enabling its publication. I am also indebted to Professors Yohanan Friedmann, Isaac Hasson, and Ella Landau-Tasseron—all of the Hebrew University of Jerusalem—and to Dr. Israel Elad-Altman of the Interdisciplinary Center of Herzliya for their erudite and useful comments. I would also like to thank my wife, Tali, my children, Einat, Amitai, and Roni, and my mother, Lili Matalon Rochen, for their encouragement in the course of the writing. Of course, all views, errors, and deficiencies in this book are completely my own.

Introduction

SINCE THE ATTACKS on New York and Washington on September 11, 2001, much has been written about the political, sociological, and religious motivation of "Islamist terrorism." The use of "Islamist," rather than "Islamic," suggest its place in a list of destructive ideologies—most recently, Nazism and communism—that have taken root during various periods in the fertile soil of Western political culture. The term also reflects a reluctance to identify acts of terrorism with the bona fide teachings of one of the world's great religions or to recognize the derivation of the jihād phenomenon from the tenets of Islam, attributing it rather to a pent-up political hostility toward the West. Some further contend that terrorism "has nothing to do with Islam," or that, if it does, it is perpetrated by "extremists" who have "hijacked Islam." An interpretation that links Islamist terrorism to authentic religious principles or cultural traits runs the risk of being branded as bigoted and Islamophobic.

It may be assumed that the great majority of Muslims in the world have no desire to embark on a jihād of any sort against the West. Moderate Muslims argue that jihād in Islam should be interpreted as a spiritual rather than a military struggle and that the paradigm of the Prophet Muhammad should inspire his followers to tolerance, leniency, love for humankind, and the rejection of terrorism.[1] But it

---

1. This argument has been extensively presented in Richard Bonney, *Jihād from Qur'an to Bin Laden* (Hampshire, UK: Palgrave-Macmillan, 2004).

is not this paradigm that inspires the self-styled mujāhidūn of the Muslim world. Another contention is that these radicals are a marginal ideological minority or a deviant cult in Islam whose interpretation of jihād is categorically rejected by orthodox Islam and, therefore, cannot gain currency among the masses of Muslims. This argument ignores the fact that there is no religious firewall between the radicals and mainstream orthodox Muslims, leaving the latter vulnerable to the absolutist arguments of the former. Much of the preaching and many of the *fatwās*—legal opinions of Islamic jurists that deal with the permissibility or prohibition of an act—emanating from mainstream Islamic circles in Mecca and Cairo cannot be easily distinguished from those of al-Qa'ida. The weakness of the moderate position is evident in the discourse among Muslim scholars, particularly since September 11 and certainly since the American operation began in Iraq.

Relying on Islamic sources of authority to justify extremism is not new. As the thirteenth-century scholar Ibn Qayyim al-Jawziyya, who serves as a source for many modern fundamentalists, put it: "As for the fanatics, they can place any problem upside down. When they turn to the *sunnah* they borrow only what corresponds to their pronouncements and contrive tricks to push away evidence that does not suit them. If they come across similarly convincing or even less convincing evidence that supports their positions, they immediately accept it and use it as an argument against their opponents."[2] What was true in the thirteenth century is true today.

Many liberal Muslims have been engaged in "cultural soul searching,"[3] an attempt to stem the tide of radicalism that, in their eyes,

2. Ibn Qayyim al-Jawziyya, *'Alām al-Muqaqqi'īn 'an Rabb il-'Alamīn* (Instruction for those who speak in the name of the Lord of the Worlds), Taha 'Abd al-Ra'uf Sa'd, ed. (Beirut: Dar al-Jil, 1973), 1:76.

3. See Abdel Rahman al-Rashed, "Almost all Terrorists are Muslim . . ." *Al-Sharq al-Awsat*, (September 4, 2004); Suleiman al-Hatlan, "Who represents Islam . . ." *Al-Watan*, (September 2004); "Arab and Muslim Reactions to the Terrorist Attack in Beslan, Russia," *MEMRI, Special Dispatch Series* 780 (2004); "Reactions to Sheikh al-Qaradhawi's Fatwā Calling for the Abduction and Killing of American Civilians

draws the Muslim world into a disastrous clash of civilizations. Some of them call for immediate reform in Islam which would uproot anachronistic beliefs that legitimize radical interpretations. Although these liberals may be spokespeople for a silent majority, they are clearly a political minority, and their religious, moral, and economic sway over their societies cannot, at the moment, overcome the combined strength of the mainstream and the radicals.

The controversy over the correlation between the doctrine of jihād and acts of terrorism has sparked a debate both in the West and within the Muslim world. On one hand, the non-Islamic diagnoses offered by many scholars and political figures include political causes (the Israeli-Arab conflict, U.S. interventionism or military presence in the gulf); cultural causes (rebellion against Western cultural colonialism); and social causes (alienation, poverty). Many warn that to uproot the phenomenon these justified grievances must be resolved. Some also point out that many religions (Judaism and Christianity included) have doctrines of "holy war" equivalent to the Islamic concept of jihād.[4] On the other hand, those who lean toward an Islamic etiology of the phenomenon point out that although terrorism—even suicide terrorism—is not an exclusively Islamic phenomenon, the majority of terrorist acts (and the most devastating of them in recent years) have been perpetrated in the name of Islam. Moreover, many societies that claim similar grievances have not given birth to religious-based ideologies justifying no-holds-barred terrorism against their perceived enemies. Therefore, to treat terrorism in Muslim societies as the consequence of political and socioeconomic factors alone does not take into account the centrality of the religious culture that allows it to flourish. The success of radical Islamic organizations in recruiting, posting, and maintaining of sleeper activists (the

in Iraq," *MEMRI, Special Dispatch Series* 794 (2004); and Mundir Badr Haloum in *Al-Safir,* in *MEMRI, Special Dispatch Series* 787 (2004). Similar headlines were printed in the Egyptian press in the wake of the attacks of 23 July in *Sharm a'Sheikh.*

4. See James Turner Johnson, *The Holy War Idea in Western and Islamic Traditions* (Philadelphia: Pennsylvania State University Press, 2002).

9/11 terrorists are a prime example) without their defecting or succumbing to the lure of Western civilization makes evident the deeply religious nature of the phenomenon.

Muslims have waged jihāds with clear political causes and goals against Western powers and others throughout the modern age. The Fulani jihāds of the eighteenth and nineteenth centuries in western Africa supported an ethnic rebellion against Hausa domination. The jihād of the Sudanese Mahdī Muhammad Ahmad against the British also Islamized an essentially political struggle. Other examples include the Chechnyan jihāds against the Russians and the ethnic Turkish-Uighur struggle against the Han Chinese throughout the nineteenth and the twentieth centuries. The Muslim Indian struggle against the British also took on the shape of a jihad under Sayid Ahmed Barlevi (1826–1831) and in the 1858 Sapoy mutiny.[5] Whatever the causes of these struggles, the moral justification and levers of public influence attending them were based not on political arguments but on Islamic principles and sources of authority, a natural outcome of the role that Islam plays in Muslim societies and of the principle that Islam is both "religion and politics" (*din wa-dawlah*).

Such jihāds, however, rarely involved individuals from other Muslim countries or spread beyond the territories in which the fighting took place. (Even the involvement of the Egyptian and Jordanian Muslim Brotherhood in the 1948 war against Israel was modest.) Until the 1980s, attempts to mobilize Muslims around the world for a jihād in one area (Palestine, Kashmir) met with only modest success. Furthermore, Islamic jihāds generally did not, until the last decades of the twentieth century, entail indiscriminate terrorism or attacks beyond the territorial boundaries of the Muslim country in which the jihad was being fought. The Soviet invasion of Afghanistan was a watershed event. It was perceived by Muslims as an essen-

---

5. For an extensive discussion of jihāds in modern times, see Bonney, *Jihād from Qur'an to Bin Laden*, pp. 172–195; and Rudolph Peters, *Islam and Colonialism: The Doctrine of Jihād in Modern History* (The Hague: Mouton, 1979), pp. 39–94.

tially defensive jihād, obliging Muslims everywhere to take part in the "general call" for liberation of Afghanistan. That jihād became an individual duty for Muslims in the attacked or occupied country, and, because of the jihādists' failure to repel the enemy, the duty then devolved to all Muslims.

This study explores the role fatwās play in Islam-motivated terrorism. These rulings provide legal and moral dispensation for acts of terrorism that are deemed to fulfill the duty of jihād. The use of fatwās to make violent action an obligation became widely known to the West when, in 1989, a fatwā issued by Ayatollah Khomeini called for the killing of Salman Rushdie, author of *The Satanic Verses*. In 1993 the Egyptian sheikh Omar 'Abd al-Rahman was tried for providing the religious justification for the first attack on the World Trade Center in 1993. In 1998, Osama bin Laden issued a fatwā calling on Muslims to wage a jihād against the United States and Israel. Since then, the number of fatwās urging jihād has increased. Although not all those who issue fatwās are qualified to do so, their influence should not be taken lightly. Many Islamist terrorists have testified that they acted on the basis of fatwās from prominent scholars.[6]

Nevertheless, the true import of the fatwā as a genuine religious instrument for motivating terrorism has not been adequately appreciated. Many Western analysts tend to dismiss fatwās as little more than cynical religious terminology applied to political propaganda. This characterization, however, does not do justice to the painstaking process of legal reasoning invested in them or the reli-

6. For example, the Saudi terrorist 'Abd Al-Rahim bin Muhammad bin 'Abdallah Al-Muteiri told *Al-'Iraqiya TV* (Iraq) on March 31, 2005 that he had acted under the influence of fatwās by twenty-six Saudi 'ulamā, and by Sheikh Yousuf Qaradawi, who had said that jihād in Iraq is a duty for all Muslims, www.memritv.org/ Transcript.asp?P1 = 62. Another Iraqi terrorist, Talal Ra'ad Suleiman Yassin, attributed his acts to fatwās by the head of the Saudi Supreme Council of 'Ulamā, 'Abd Al-'Aziz Aal Al-Sheikh. *Al-'Iraqiya TV* (Iraq), 9 March 2005, www.memritv.org/ Transcript.asp?P1 = 602.

gious gravity with which their authors and their target audience treat them. To understand fatwās properly, one must recognize the centrality in Islam of law as a regulator of all aspects of life, and the link between the legalistic and casuistic methodology of Islamic jurisprudence and the moral issues they strive to regulate. Because under normal circumstances an act of terror would be considered morally repugnant, legally prohibited, and punishable in the hereafter, legal and moral justifications, and clear guidelines, are the *sine qua non* for the believing Muslim who engages in it.

The Qur'an (2:16) cautions Muslims that "it may be that you dislike a thing that is good for you and like a thing that is bad for you. Allah knows but you do not know." During the life of the Prophet, the Muslim community could turn to him for what "Allah knows but you do not know" and behave accordingly. However, in Sunni Islam at least, no human after the Prophet may presume to transmit the authoritative will of Allah. Sanctioning an act of violence or war as something desirable to Allah devolved first to the caliph or imām or, in his absence, to the 'ulamā, whose task it became to find analogies between current dilemmas and the explicit or implicit examples of the Prophet and to rule accordingly.

Based as it is on the minutest behaviors of the Prophet, Islamic jurisprudence naturally delves into one of his primary occupations—conducting jihād. The rise of the terrorist jihād movement in the last two decades of the twentieth century has been accompanied by a renaissance in legal analysis that aims to anchor jihād as a lawful religious obligation, define clear guidelines for waging it, and, thus, provide moral and legal sanctions for acts of terrorism. These contemporary fatwās specify the current status and area of application of the state of jihād; elaborate the necessary conditions for jihād; classify the "infidels" against whom jihād must be waged; determine who must participate in jihād and how; establish the legitimate means and the legitimate targets of jihād; and defend the legitimacy of suicide attacks and even of the use of nuclear weapons. Although the discussions in these fatwās may seem casuistic, they hold far-reaching implications for believing Muslims, subordinating questions that are commonly deemed moral and ethical to the legal analysis.

The purpose of this book is to present and analyze the role of radical fatwās in providing the legal and moral justification for Islamist terrorism, and to examine the scope of their influence particularly in contrast to that of moderate Islamic interpretations. Drawing on a large body of contemporary fatwās and legal tracts collected for more than a decade from Islamic centers, bookstores, mosques, journals, and the Internet, I explore a wide sampling of the religious and legal thinking in various Islamic circles regarding the jihād. The fatwās' authors are Islamic scholars of various leanings, mainly from the Arab world. In examining these writings, I have also searched for fatwās by prominent Islamic religious scholars that contradict the radical interpretation.

Fatwās are not the only way to transmit radical ideas about jihād. A number of scholars have produced articles and books analyzing the law of jihād that present a cogent justification for violence. Others preach to wide audiences in mosques, in radio and TV broadcasts, and on audio- and videotapes. Many of these echo the legal arguments justifying terror in the fatwās, and they play an important role in mobilizing support for terror. But this book concentrates on the legal thinking of Sunni Islam, the dominant branch, in light of the influence that fatwās on jihād have had in Sunni fundamentalist circles, on the mujāhidūn movement in Afghanistan, and on the international jihād movement, as embodied in the al-Qa'ida network. This is not to suggest that fatwās in Shiite Islam are less important or less influential than those of the Sunni world. But the structure of authority in the Sunni world differs in many crucial areas from that of Shiite Islam, with its emphasis on the prerogative of the descendant of the fourth caliph, 'Ali—the Imām—who is in "occultation" (*ghaybah*) and will return in the future to enforce justice, and its system of accepted "sources of authority" (*marja'iyah*), making it difficult to draw comprehensive generalizations relevant to both systems.

The source language of most of the texts in this study is Arabic.

Many fatwās, however, are promulgated on the Internet in a number of languages, showing that their authors and disseminators perceive their target audience not only as Arabs and Islamic-educated Muslims who can read Arabic but also as speakers of Urdu, Bahasa, Farsi, and English, that is, UK-born Pakistanis and other second-generation Muslims in the United States, United Kingdom, and other English-speaking countries. For the sake of accuracy I have used, where available, the English translations provided by the authors of the fatwās, comparing them with the Arabic originals. In other cases, the translation is my own (which readers should recognize as "unauthorized," in the sense that my English renditions have not been approved by the authors of those texts). Translations of verses from the Qur'an have been taken from different versions, and occasionally I have offered my own renderings. Because the terminology of Islamic law is Arabic, in some cases, after defining a term, I give the Arabic along with simplified transliteration.

Finally, a caveat: The contemporary fatwās discussed here are only the latest link in a chain of Islamic philosophy, theology, and legal thinking that stretches from the dawn of Islam in the seventh century to the present. This study draws on but does not delve deeply into the vast sea of Islamic law, which consists of a prodigious body of legal texts; esoteric discussions of relevant verses of the Qur'an and the collection of stories about the Prophet related by his companions (*ḥadīth*); and practical fatwās on matters relating to the conduct of jihād, conditions for initiating jihād (*jus ad bellum*), and the laws of war during a jihād (*jus in bello*). I have supplied some of this background in footnotes, but a full discussion is beyond the scope of this work.

CHAPTER 1

'Ulamā and Fatwās in Islam

I SLAM is a nomocracy. It is based on government by immutable law, offering the believer not only revelation of divine will but also a highly detailed legal code that provides order, instruction, and indeed balm for the malaise of the human condition by regulating all aspects of human behavior, both private and collective. More than merely requiring orthodoxy, or correct belief, of its followers, it requires orthopraxy, or correct practice, particularly in public, in accordance with the Islamic legal code (*shari'ah*). It is this code that the leaders and members of the *ummah* (the Islamic nation or community) are expected to apply on a day-to-day basis.

A basic premise of Western legal philosophy is "Whatever is not forbidden is permitted."[1] Although this principle can be formally deduced from the fundamentals of Islam,[2] in practice Islamic law tends to view the entire scope of human behavior—private and public, mo-

---

1. The principle is attributed to Friedrich von Schiller. However, the "silence principle," which stipulates that things not permitted are forbidden, was the subject of debate in early Christianity.

2. See Yousuf Qaradawi, *Al-ḥalāl wa-al-ḥarām fī-Islām* (The permitted and forbidden in Islam), Chapter 1, www.qaradawi.net/site/topics/article.asp?cu_no=2&item_no=15&version=1&template_id=5&parent_id=1. This was also the explicit opinion of King Ibn Sa'ud, the founder of Saudi Arabia, which he used to legitimize the introduction of Western methods and technology into the kingdom.

rality and immorality—as matters to be regulated by the precepts of shari'ah: "the whole duty of Mankind, moral and pastoral theology and ethics, high spiritual aspiration and detailed ritualistic and formal observances; it encompasses all aspects of public and private law, hygiene, and even courtesy and good manners."[3] All religious and moral issues can be deduced from shari'ah through casuistic analysis, and clear instructions can be given regarding right and wrong. The sources of shari'ah are primarily the Qur'an and the exemplary behavior of the Prophet (the sunnah) as related in the books of ḥadīths. Together they provide the Muslim with a clear prescription for the "straight path," which calls for meticulous imitating of the ways of the Prophet and his Companions as recounted in the Qur'an and the ḥadīth, reinstating the "Rule of Allah," and rejecting any "innovation" (bid'a) that contradicts the sunnah.

Hence, ideally, all conceivable acts can be classified on a scale ranging from a duty (farḍ or wājib)[4] to that which is desirable or encouraged (mustaḥabb, mandūb, or sunnah), permissible (ḥalāl, mubaḥ, or ja'iz), discouraged or reprehensible (makrūh), or forbidden (ḥarām). This classification of human behavior means that if the believer performs all his religious duties, he will inherit paradise; if he fails to do so or does that which is forbidden, he may be condemned to hell for eternity or until the Day of Judgment.

Because orthodox Sunni Islam never officially relegated anachronistic elements of the religion to a historical context and replaced them with updated concepts, all texts and concepts remain valid. Tools for such anachronization, though, do exist. Because the surahs of the Qur'an were revealed at different times during the mission

3. S.G. Vesey-Fitzgerald, "Nature and Sources of the Sharia," in Majid Khadduri and Herbert Liebesny, eds., *Law in the Middle East* (Washington, D.C.: Middle East Institute, 1955), p. 85.

4. Some jurists distinguish between farḍ and wājib. The former is a duty imposed in the Qur'an. The latter is a duty that derives from legal rulings, and therefore its omission is not as grave a sin.

of the Prophet, some schools of Islamic jurisprudence recognize the principle of abrogation (*naskh*) according to which an earlier abrogated text is replaced by a later *abrogating* text. A related tool is *particularization* (*takhsīs*)—linking a specific statement in the Qur'an to a specific (historic) event, thus voiding it of its general implications. This logic is extensively discussed in medieval texts dealing with the "circumstances of revelation," "intentions," or "wisdom of the text" (*asbāb al-nuzūl, maqasid, hikmat al-nass*). Scholars have never reached a consensus, however, regarding either the mechanism of abrogation or the hierarchy of verses (determining which abrogate which). Even for those who accept those mechanisms, the possibility of abrogation was not extended past the lifetime of the Prophet.[5] Islam also recognizes the mechanism of *ijtihād*, the discretion of learned scholars (*mujtāhidūn*) to make new judgments based on their understanding of the spirit of the sacred texts.[6]

The "straight path" of Islam is a public road, not a private one, and a Muslim cannot walk it alone. Islam is, in essence, a communal religion with a strong sense of interdependence. Therefore, a central obligation in Islam is to "command right and forbid evil"[7]: a Muslim must set other Muslims on the "right path." Wherever he comes across Muslims contradicting Islam, he must correct them, prefera-

5. The modern school of Islamic thought that endeavors to adapt fiqh to modern life in the West (*fiqh al-aqaliyat*—law of minorities) tends to embrace these ideas and to renew the legitimacy of independent "exegisis" (ijtihād) in a manner reminiscent of the medieval rationalist school of the Mu'tazila. See Shamai Fishman, "Fiqh al-Aqaliyat: A Religious Solution for Muslims Residing in the West," unpublished paper.

6. See Wael Hallaq, *Islamic Legal Theories*, pp. 68–74, 45–46, 195, 112, 180–184.

7. This principle (*al-amr bil-maarūf wa-al-nahy 'an al-munkar*) is based on Qur'an (3:104), "Let there be one Nation among you, commanding right and forbidding evil," and Qur'an (3:104), "You are the best nation, commanding right and forbidding evil." For an extensive study of this principle, see Michael Cook, *Forbidding Wrong in Islam* (Cambridge: Cambridge University Press, 2003).

bly by hand, and, failing that, by tongue, and, failing that, in his heart.[8] Taken to its extreme, and combined with the ideal of Islam as including all aspects of human life, this moral tenet—a pillar of modern Islamist radicalism—makes it the individual responsibility of each Muslim to wage jihād.

But in what does this jihad consist? Because Muhammad was the "seal of the prophets," and because God does not speak directly with mankind, it is critical to determine what is a duty and what is forbidden, and what is the right that is commanded and what is the evil that must be forbidden? Even when good and evil are clearly identified, how should good be achieved and evil avoided? In any ethical system these are difficult tasks, but in religious ethical systems based on sacred texts attributed to revelation, the difficulty increases because such texts are esoteric and ambiguous. They frequently support thesis and antithesis, moral positions and their diametrically opposed alternatives. The ambiguity is compounded by believers' faith that they are created by a higher Being of infinite wisdom. Sophisticated and circuitous interpretations which are thought to attest to that infinite wisdom are often preferred to simplified readings.

Moreover, the poetic style of the Qur'an, its complex structure, with later verses seemingly contradicting earlier ones, and the strength or authenticity of the various ḥadīths attributed to the Prophet and his Companions, make understanding the will of God an arduous task. The laity does not have "the time, the training, or

8. So explains a ḥadīth which quotes the Prophet as saying "He who amongst you sees something abominable should modify it with the help of his hand; and if he has not strength enough to do it, then he should do it with his tongue, and if he has not strength enough to do it, (even) then he should (abhor it) from his heart, and that is the least of faith." *Sahih Muslim* (*Kitāb al-Imān*) Book 1, No. 79. It is interesting that the Lebanese Shiite scholar Ayatollah Mahdī Shams a-Din presents the priorities the other way around: preventing with the hand is the last resort and only after the first two have been tried. Shams-a-Din, Ayatollah Sheikh Muhammad Mahdī, *Fiqh al-'unf al-Mosalah fi-l-Islam* (The law of armed violence in Islam) (Beirut: al-Mowassat al-dawliya lil-dirasat wa-al-nashr, 2001), p. 105.

perhaps the capacity to thoroughly study and analyze the indicators
. . . the responsibility of the laity is to imitate the jurists.'"[9] Therefore,
the jurists (*fuqaha* [sing. *faqīh*]) or scholars ('ulamā) must interpret
and hand down the guidelines for all matters concerning Islam,
whether religious, moral, or political. A Muslim's duty to seek guidance from the scholars and obey them is reiterated in many fatwās
by those very scholars and is a primary source of their spiritual, social,
and political power.

The 'ulamā in Muslim societies traditionally occupied a variety of
roles: a legislative one that, by interpreting the sources of the law,
created new duties and prohibitions; a judicial one that passed judgment on violators of the law; and a political one that provided religious legitimacy to the leadership. During most of Islamic history,
the jurists and the rulers complemented each other: the clerics provided rulers with legitimacy and the rulers provided clerics with security and material benefits. Occasional conflicts arose between the
two, which usually resulted in a new and better modus vivendi.[10]

In the modern age, and in the modern secular nation-state, however, political leaders lost their religious legitimacy (in many cases
not seeking it), and the clerical establishment was largely divested of
its social and political role.

Although the relationship between such secular Muslim regimes
and their "house 'ulamā" has often been uneasy, the most prominent Islamic establishment—the prestigious al-Azhar in Cairo—
flexibly maneuvered between popular sentiment and the powers-
that-be. In 1798, al-Azhar's leading scholars went from extensive in-
teractions with the French to rebellion against them. Similarly, dur-

9. Khaled Abou El Fadl, *Speaking in God's Name: Islamic Law, Authority and
Women* (Oxford: Oneworld, 2001), p. 51.

10. For an in-depth analysis of the relationship between 'ulamā and rulers, see
Khaled Abou El Fadl, *Rebellion and Violence in Islamic Law* (Cambridge: Cambridge University Press, 2001), pp. 8–31. For a concise overview, see Miriam Netzer,
"One Voice? The Crisis of Legal Authority in Islam," *Al-Nakhlah* (Spring, 2004):
art. 6.

ing the decades of Israeli–Arab conflict, the institution showed itself
highly sensitive to public opinion.[11] Modern Muslim regimes have
used ʻulamā-issued fatwās to legitimize their policies, bolster their
Islamic credentials against domestic opponents, and mobilize support against foreign enemies. Historic examples include the ʻulamā's
calls to rally to the Ottoman Caliphate (December 1914) in World
War I; the Lebanese Shiite leader Mussa Sadr's call to recognize the
Alawites as Shiite Muslims; and the fatwā issued by the Cairo Academy of Islamic Research (majmaʼ al-buhuth al-Islamiya) in November 1977 (in the wake of President Anwar Sadat's visit to Jerusalem)
ruling that the purpose of jihād was no longer to destroy Israel but
to establish a Palestinian state in the areas occupied in 1967.[12] The
regime in Saudi Arabia used a fatwā issued by the Council of Senior
ʻUlamā to sanction the use of force against the group that occupied
the Grand Mosque in Mecca in 1979, and, in the wake of the Iraqi
invasion of Kuwait, to justify a Western intervention against another
Muslim country.

The political implications of the issuing of fatwās have caused
many Muslim countries to form "fatwā committees" or "fatwā councils," either within the traditional Islamic academies or separate
from them.[13] Those bodies are usually composed of senior clerics

11. Elena Aragita, "Al-Azhar in the Post 9/11 Era," ISIM Newsletter 14 (June
2004): 46–47.

12. Peters, Islam and Colonialism, p. 107.

13. Muhammad al-Atawneh, "Fatwās and Iftaʼ in Saudi Arabia: A Study of Islamic Legal Thought, 1971–2000" (Unpublished doctoral dissertation, Ben Gurion
University, Israel, 2004), pp. 15–43. Examples of such committees include "The European Council for Fatwā and Research"; "The Fiqh Council of North America";
"The Islamic Fiqh Academy in India"; "Islamic Research Academy"; and "Dār al-
fatwā." In Egypt this function is embodied in the ancient structure of al-Azhar. In
Saudi Arabia, a State Grand Mufti and Dār al-Iftaʼ wal-Ishrāf ʻAla al-Shuūn al-Dīnīi-
yya (House of Fatwā and Supervision of Religious Affairs) was established for the
first time only in 1952 when the muftis were incorporated into the ruling system
and made partners to policies and political decisions. In 1971, the Saudi regime
reorganized the fatwā system in order to enhance its control over the muftis and
created two new bodies: Hayat Kibār al-ʻUlamā (Board of Senior Ulama) and Al-

whose purpose is to provide Islamic legitimacy to political decisions and secular laws. Their authority, however, has steadily declined in the face of challenges from popular radical scholars and governments' increasing efforts to exert control. The religious establishment has lately responded to the challenge of the non-establishment ulamā by producing edicts prohibiting the issuing of fatwās by "non-authorized" clerics.

Relations between the regimes and their 'ulamā differ from one country to another. The Saudi royal family has lost much of its control over the rank-and-file 'ulamā. Since 9/11, the number of fatwās issued by radical clerics in the kingdom has been on the rise. As a result, the government decreed that only authorized 'ulamā can issue fatwās and that only the government can issue rulings on jihād. For the same reason, Kuwait established a committee to coordinate and approve fatwās. In Egypt, where the Fatwā Committee of al-Azhar has issued a wide range of fatwās calling for everything from a boycott of the United States to suicide terrorism, the government has tried to avoid compromising al-Azhar's independence. Syria, in contrast, is less concerned about promoting the independence of its own "court 'ulamā." Less blatantly, Jordan continues to maintain control over its religious establishment.

Islamic jurisprudence (*fiqh*) is the mechanism by which a scholar brings the principles of shari'ah to bear on practice. It results in the delivery of a fatwā, written or oral, on a specific subject that dispels uncertainty and shows a clear path for behavior. Traditionally, a fatwā can only be given by a scholar whose knowledge of shari'ah is wide enough to be considered a *mufti*. The classic fatwā consists of a question and a response. The fatwā's formal language must define the legal issue that the query raises, refer to previous relevant rulings, and provide a clear guide for the petitioner so that he may avoid any unwitting sin.

Lajnah al-Daimah Li-l-Buḥuth al-'Ilmiyya wal-Iftā' (Permanent Committee for Scientific Research and Legal Opinion).

A fatwā must be based on the sources of fiqh, which include, first and foremost, the Qur'an and the sunnah. Also taken into consideration are logical analogies (*qiyas*), the consensus of the 'ulamā (*ijma'*) or, in the extreme case, ijtihad,[14] all of which are at the discretion of the 'ulamā. Such discretion may also take into account "opinion" (*ra'y, nazar*), preferences (*istihsān*), pragmatic determination of public interest (*maslahah*), necessity (*darūra*), or even the existence of external "compulsion" (*ikrah*) as an extenuating factor. One far-reaching interpretation of the intent of shari'ah is that of the medieval jurist Abu Ishaq al-Shatibi, who derived all its elements from three categories of human good: *daruriyyāt* (necessities), *hajiyyāt* (alleviation of hardship), and *tahsiniyyāt* (improving the human condition).[15] Most fatwās, though, rely on precedents set by the mujtā-hidūn of early Islam and the codex of existing fatwās. Early in Islam's history, ijtihād began to wane, and by the tenth century the "gates of ijtihād" were considered closed for most of Sunni Islam, although it continued to be practiced by a few Sunni scholars (particularly Shafi'i scholars of Southeast Asia) and Shiites. Reluctance to resort to ijtihād left most of Sunni Islam without a way of relegating a tenet or text to obsolescence. Theological pondering and exegesis of the original sources gave way to "following tradition" (*taqlīd*) and specious arguments were developed that would allow tenth-century rulings to be implemented in twentieth- and twenty-first-century cases.

The laity's reliance on legal dispensations from 'ulamā raises the question of personal accountability. Does a scholar who provides an erroneous fatwā, or a Muslim who follows him, commit a sin? This

14. The early mujtahidun founded the four major Sunnite schools of jurisprudence (*madhab*, pl. *madhāhib*): Hanafi, Maliki, Shafi'i, Hanbali (in addition to the Shiite Ja'afari school and the smaller Zaydi, Ibadi, and Ismai'ili schools). Any Muslim may adhere to any one of them and each school may provide equally binding but diverse rulings on a variety of issues. Thomas Patrick Hughes, *Dictionary of Islam* (New Delhi: Munshiram Manoharlal Publishers, 1885), pp. 197–199.

15. Wael B. Hallaq, A *History of Islamic Legal Theories: An Introduction to Sunni usul al-fiqh* (Cambridge: Cambridge University Press, 1997), pp. 167–174.

question is particularly relevant to acts of violence which, if committed in the context of a legitimate jihād, may be a primary duty, and if not, a severe sin. If the misleading opinion is intentional, its author has committed the heinous sin of *istiḥlāl*—"permitting that which (Allah) forbade" or *istiḥram*—"forbidding that which (Allah) permitted" (Qur'an 9:37). Islam, however, is exceptionally tolerant of the honest mistakes of scholars (a saying attributed to the Prophet asserts that "my people are never mistaken"). The differences of opinion among scholars in Islam's early days gave rise to the idea that the ijtihād is a commendable deed. According to ḥadīth attributed to the Prophet, "every mujtāhid is correct." If a scholar performs ijtihād in good faith, he is rewarded by Allah—with one reward if he is mistaken, and with two rewards if he is right. Differences of opinion are considered legitimate and even "a benefit to the ummah." This pluralism has its drawbacks: although clear lines are drawn by radicals against interpretations that are too lenient, the respect for differences of opinion frequently gives legitimacy to radical interpretations.[16]

A Sunni Muslim who poses a question to a scholar does not necessarily have to accept his ruling; he may seek a second opinion. Often, however, the petitioner knows in advance what the general sense of the fatwā will be because he is strongly affiliated with a certain scholar and shares his general religious worldview.

The lay Muslim's subordination to the 'ulamā is compounded for the radical movements. Their members may pledge an oath of fealty or allegiance (*bay'a*) to their leaders, whose titles—Amir (commander), Muraqib (overseer), Murshid (guide), or even Mahdī (messiah)—reflect such a relationship. The oath, derived from pledges of fealty to tribal leaders or the Muslim caliph, indicates acceptance of the leader as both spiritual guide and temporal leader. His fatwā

16. Khaled Abou El Fadl, *And God Knows the Soldiers: The Authoritative and Authoritarian in Islamic Discourse* (New York: University Press of America, 2001), pp. 24–25.

then is not only a juridical opinion but an operational diktat, reminiscent of Gnostic sects in Christianity, characterized by an all-powerful and omniscient leader with a unique interpretation of reality and a clear path to salvation.

The characteristics described above relate to Sunni Islam. Formally at least, Shiite 'ulamā wield even greater sway over their followers than their Sunni counterparts. Shiite Islam never closed "the gates of ijtihād." Rather, it expanded its scope and placed it in the hands of a number of living authorities. The highest religious authority in Islam is that of a *marja' taqlīd*, or "model of emulation." Every Shiite Muslim is expected to follow such a model, but given that there is a large number of maraja' hailing from a variety of backgrounds and countries, a Shiite Muslim may follow only one who is living. When a marja' dies, his followers must accept the authority of another marja'. This principle operates on the collective level as well. If all the 'ulamā of a certain generation accept a given ruling by consensus, such a decision is only binding on that generation and not in the future.

CHAPTER 2

The Mechanism of the Jihād Fatwā

F ATWĀS have been employed by rebels and insurgents across the Muslim world against westernized regimes' presumed heresy and foreign domination. This was true, for example of the Wahhabis in the Arabian Peninsula (1881–85), the Mahdī in Sudan (1881–1885), and by Muslims in India against the British (1881) and in Indonesia against the Dutch (1948). The 1991 Gulf War enlarged the U.S. presence in the Persian Gulf, particularly in Saudi Arabia, and exacerbated the view in the Muslim world of Saudi Arabia as a Muslim land occupied (at least culturally and morally) by infidels. In Afghanistan the defeat of the Soviet Union (and its subsequent demise) made clear to the veterans of the Afghani jihād that the Muslims have the power, by virtue of their faith and the fervor of jihād, to expel the infidels and regain Muslim lands for the Muslim ummah.

But the jihād's mechanism and logic had to be regulated by scholarly fatwās, which vary according to the supplicant, the source of the issues raised, and the identity and affiliation of the respondents. Some involve bona fide questions posed by devout Muslims confused by the apparent contradiction between the legal reasoning of the clerics who call for jihād and the conventional morality of modern society, not to mention their own personal scruples. The defendants in the first World Trade Center trial explained their reliance on Sheikh Omar 'Abd el-Rahman, by saying that his approval was necessary "whenever one did something 'basically unlawful,' which would be wrong unless the 'mission was under the flag of God and his messenger.'"[1] Many other fatwās, however, are clearly politically initiated: the questions are either invented or invited by the responding scholar to provide him the opportunity to present his legal reasoning on some aspect of jihād.

The authors of the fatwās dealing with jihād come from diverse backgrounds. Some are scholars who provide their flock with fatwās on a wide range of issues. Others are "political 'ulamā" and leaders of political fundamentalist movements who are not seen in the wider Islamic world as having authority to provide fatwās but are accepted as authorities by their followers.[2] Furthermore, not all fatwās are prepared by individuals. Some are issued by traditional Islamic institutions of higher education, such as al-Azhar in Egypt or fatwā committees affiliated with Muslim communities or with Muslim governments. Many fundamentalist movements (for example, the Muslim Brotherhood and similar groups) also have their own fatwā committees (or councils) that turn out politically motivated fatwās on a regular basis, though some defer regularly to external sources of authority.[3] In the final analysis, the influence of the fatwās derives first from the larger religious authority and then from its author.

The sources for ruling in these fatwās are, for the most part, the Qur'an and ḥadīth. Jihād-oriented scholars with Salafi–Wahhabi or Hanbali leanings claim to rely almost exclusively on these sources. However, because ijtihād has also been revived—officially or de

1. *United States v. Rahman*, 189 F.3d 88 (1999).

2. A prime example is Osama bin Ladin himself. Others of this type are Sheikh Omar Abu Qatada and Sheikh Yousuf Qaradawi. The leader of the Hizb al-Tahrir, Taqi a-din Nabahani, was considered by his followers as a "mujtahid mutlaq" (absolute mujtahid).

3. The Muslim Brotherhood in Jordan has been extremely prolific over the last few years in promulgating political fatwās. The Palestinian Hamas, on the other hand, has no homegrown religious authority and frequently turns to the Egyptian and Jordanian Muslim Brotherhood for guidance on fiqh.

facto—in the radical Islamic movements, the radical ʿulamā have great latitude in their rulings.[4]

Most fatwās concerning jihād originate in the Arabic-speaking world (specifically from ʿulamā coming from the gulf countries, Egypt, Jordan, and Palestine). However fatwās of this nature have been issued in other parts of the Muslim world as well, particularly Pakistan, the Philippines, and Indonesia.[5] All these Muslim societies are engaged in struggles with their non-Muslim neighbors over the independence (Kashmir, Mindanao) or autonomy (Aceh) of Muslim territory, though Arab Islam is predominant even in such non-Arab theaters. Many ʿulamā in those countries who issue fatwās calling for jihād are either of Arab origin or have studied for years in the higher Islamic academies of the Arab world (al-Azhar in Egypt or in Mecca), as evidenced by their style and reasoning. One example of such fatwās is a series issued by muftis in Saudi Arabia (April 6, 2000) that legitimized the paramilitary group Laskar Jihād, which operated against Christians in the Molucca.[6] Outside the Arab world, the second fountainhead of influence on jihād jurisprudence comes from Pakistan. This source, however, is intimately linked to the Arab world. serving as a conduit for Islamic concepts.

The fatwās examined in this book are not all the works of outstanding scholars whose legal discretion is above reproach, for one characteristic of radical Islamic movements is that political leaders arrogate the right to issue fatwās. I do not discuss here the causes of the breakdown in scholarly authority in the Muslim world that

4. It is ironic that the drive for revival of ijtihād in the modern era, which was promoted by nineteenth-century reformists such as Muhammad ʾAbdou and Rashid Rida, gave rise to the incorporation of ijtihād both in the fundamentalist movements of the Muslim world (such as the Muslim Brotherhood) and in the reformist movements of Southeast Asia (the Mohammadiya and Nahdlatul Ulama (NU) in Indonesia). Giora Eliraz, *Islam in Indonesia: Modernism, Radicalism, and the Middle East Dimension* (Brighton, UK: Sussex Academic Press, 2004), pp. 2–3, 18–25.

5. Nico J.G. Kaptein, *The Voice of the "Ulama": Fatwās and Religious Authority in Indonesia* (Singapore: Institute of Southeast Asian Studies, 2004).

6. Ibid., p. 15.

encouraged this phenomenon or the historic precedents of commanders acting in lieu of the 'ulamā in interpreting shari'ah. The end result is, in any case, a popularization of jurisprudence.

The information age has opened up new channels by which the devout Muslim can acquire religious instruction without coming in direct contact with the scholar or sheikh he is consulting. A Muslim can now send a query to a learned sheikh by e-mail and receive a ruling directly or on the public website dedicated to such fatwās. These websites vary according to the leanings of the institution they represent and the personalities of the sheikhs involved. Some establishment sites represent renowned Islamic institutions or prominent individual sheikhs and provide general Islamic instruction for the mainstream orthodox Muslim, including responses to queries on the rules and regulations of jihād. Others include religious instruction and fatwās almost exclusively dedicated to the issue of jihād. Those sites do not always provide the identity of the supplicant or the sheikh who issues the fatwā, thus compromising the authority of such fatwās.[7] Online fatwās are often recycled. Questions that have already been raised and answered are reposted, and the response posted with it as if it were given on that date. As a result, occasionally a prominent sheikh's fatwā has been posted after the sheikh's death.

These fatwās range over every subject imaginable. Some questions are directed to radical sheikhs in hopes of receiving dispensation for acts of jihād while others, posed by moderate Muslims to moderate sheikhs, anticipate moderate responses. Yet there are a number of common issues:

1. *What is the definition, current implementation, and area of application of the state of jihād?* This gives rise to many related questions. Is jihād one of the "pillars" or "roots" of Islam? Does it necessarily imply military war, or can it be perceived as

---

7. See Gary Bunt, *Islam in the Digital Age: E-Jihād, Online Fatwās and Cyber Islamic Environments* (London: Pluto Press, 2003), pp. 135–60.

a duty to spread Islam through preaching or even as the moral struggle between one's soul and Satan? If war, then what are the necessary conditions for jihād? Does a state of jihād currently exist between *dār al-Islām* (the land of Islam) and *dār al-ḥarb* (the land of war of the infidels)? And how can one define dār al-Islām today, in the absence of a caliphate? Is the rest of the world automatically defined as dār al-ḥarb, with which a state of jihād exists, or do the treaties and diplomatic relations between Muslim countries and infidel countries (including the United Nations) change this?

2. *Who must participate in jihād, and how?* Is jihād a personal duty for each and every Muslim under all circumstances or a collective duty that can be performed only under Islamic leadership (an imam, caliph, or emir)? Is it a duty for women? For minors? May a Muslim refrain from supporting his attacked brethren or obey a non-Muslim secular law that prohibits him from supporting other Muslims in their struggle?

3. *How should the jihād be fought (jus in bello)?* The questions in this area relate to (a) the definition of a legitimate target, whether it is permissible to kill noncombatant civilians— women, children, elderly, and clerics; protected non-Muslims in Muslim countries, local non-Muslims or tourists whose visas may be interpreted as Islamic guarantees of passage; or Muslim bystanders? (b) the legitimacy of suicide attacks in the light of the severe prohibition on a Muslim taking his own life and yet the promise of rewards in the afterlife for the attacker who dies in a jihād; (c) the weapons and tactics that may be used (hijacking planes? killing hostages?); (d) the status of a Muslim who aids the infidels against other Muslims; and (e) the authority to implement capital punishment in the absence of a caliph.

4. *How should jihād be funded?* This subject concerns the transfer of tithes (*zakāt*) collected in a community for jihād, the pre-

cepts of war booty, and the fifth (*khoms*) of the spoils that must be handed over to the public treasury.

5. *What is the proper behavior of a Muslim toward nonbelievers (kuffār)?* Is it permissible to support the kuffār by purchasing their products, performing acts that call for loyalty to their countries, serving in their military, spying for them, and so on?

Most of the fatwās discussed here are general requests for guidance, not specific cases. Once a fatwā has been issued legitimizing a certain category, however, there is no need to obtain further dispensation for specific acts that fall under it. Nevertheless, operational fatwās are found in radical Islamic groups. These may be directed toward certain individuals and declare him an apostate—a sin that entails a death sentence according to many scholars, such as the fatwās against Salman Rushdi (UK), Farag Foda (Egypt), and Taslima Nassreen (Bangladesh).[8] They may also be directed against impersonal targets such as international organizations, buildings, and so on. Operational fatwās have also come to light in investigations of radical Islamic organizations in Jordan and other Muslim countries, and more recently in the activities of Abu Mus'ab al-Zarqawi in Iraq.[9] Some operational fatwās are oral and lack the detail of many of the fatwās that deal with matters of principle. A jurist who issues

8. Farag Foda was murdered in June 1992 after a group of establishment 'ulamā from *al-Azhar* adopted a previous fatwā by Sheikh al-Azhar Jadd al-Haqq that determined that secularist writers, Foda among them, are enemies of Islam. A similar fatwā was issued by a popular preacher, Sheikh Mohammad al-Ghazalli. The assassins claimed in their defense that they merely executed the sentence that was issued by al-Azhar. Al-Afif al-Akhdhar, "*Al-Islamiyūn wa-al-Muthaqifūn: Mashrou' idtihād*" (The Islamists and the intellectuals: a plan of suppression), www.rezgar.com/debat/show.art.asp?t = 2&aid = 8336.

9. A recent case that was exposed in the Jordanian courts is that of 'Abd Shehadah al-Tahawi, who studied in Saudi Arabia and returned to Jordan to form a radical group. Members of the group petitioned him on various matters regarding their *jihād* plans: travel to Iraq for attacks there, attacks inside Jordan, etc. *Al-Ghur* (Jordan), 10 January 2005.

a fatwā does not necessarily have to disclose the evidence on which his ruling is based, though he must have the evidence and be willing to defend it if challenged by competent scholars.

Operational fatwās were issued by the Egyptian leader of the Gama'ah Islamiyya, Sheikh 'Omar 'Abd al-Rahman, for the assassination of President Sadat, for the first attack on the World Trade Center in New York in 1993, and for the attack on foreign tourists in Luxor, Egypt, in 1977. Abd al-Rahman was convicted for his involvement in the first World Trade Center bombing because he, "as a cleric and the group's leader . . . was entitled to dispense fatwās, religious opinions on the holiness of an act, to members of the group, sanctioning proposed courses of conduct and advising them whether the acts would be in furtherance of jihād." One of the other terrorists involved in the same attack had proposed to the sheikh bombing UN headquarters. Weighing the pros and cons, the sheikh ruled that, although the fact that Muslim delegates might be killed in the process does not make it a prohibited act, the possibility of causing harm to Muslims requires the search for an alternative plan.[10]

10. Steve Emerson, *American Jihād: The Terrorists Living Among Us* (New York: The Free Press, 2003), p. 49; and *United States v. Rahman*, 189 F.3d 88 (1999.)

CHAPTER 3

The House of Islam versus the House of War

T HE traditional Islam partition of the world into two clear entities, dār al-Islām and dār al-ḥarb—literally, "the abode of Islam" and "the abode of war"—is well known. These are not the only categories known to Islamic political thought, however, for early jurisprudence took into consideration the dangers of inflexibility. As the Islamic state crystallized, a variety of distinctions tempered the original dichotomy with a dose of realpolitik.

One such is *dār al-ʿahd* (the abode of treaty, also referred to as the abode of peace—*dār al-ṣulh*), a country with which the Muslims have a treaty, and which usually pays tribute. Another is *dār al-ḥiyad* (the abode of neutrality), which became necessary in early Islam in light of a ḥadīth in which the Prophet enjoined Muslims to leave the Christians of Abyssinia (Ethiopia) alone as long as they did not attack Muslims.[1] De facto exemption from jihād was also accorded to Cyprus because of its location between the Muslim world and Byzantium.[2] The medieval scholar Ibn Taymiyya, revered by many modern radical movements for his rulings on jihād, distinguished between

1. Majid Khadduri, *War and Peace in the Law of Islam* (Baltimore: Johns Hopkins Press, 1955), pp. 256–58.
2. Ibid., p. 267.

the "abode of war" and the "abode of non-war heresy" (*dār kufr ghayr ḥarb*).[3]

The growth of Muslim communities in non-Muslim countries during the last decades of the twentieth century has accentuated old dilemmas and created new ones. In response, modern scholars have reclassified their views on non-Muslims and non-Muslim countries:

1. The most radical view virtually redefines dār al-Islām as any country that is ruled by shari'ah; all others are dār al-ḥarb. Because all Muslim countries are, in this view, ruled by corrupt apostate regimes, they have ceased to be Muslim. Their regimes are kāfir (nonbelieving) and their citizens sunk in a state of pagan ignorance (*jāhiliyya*). A variation of this view, held by the leader of the Muhajirun movement,[4] maintains that the concept of dār al-Islām and dār al-ḥarb are no longer relevant, as dār al-Islām implies the existence of the caliphate and dār al-ḥarb cannot exist without dār al-Islām. Nevertheless, when Muslim land is occupied by kuffār, it becomes dār al-ḥarb, or *dār al-ghasab* (usurped land).[5]

2. The classic fundamentalist view, held by most Wahhabi, Salafi, and Hanbali 'ulamā and most jihād movements, reverts to the sharp dichotomy between dār al-Islām and dār al-ḥarb, which is the basis of the rulings on jihād by most radical scholars against secular Muslim regimes. This view also prohibits leaving dār al-Islām for dār al-ḥarb and obliges the faithful to emigrate from dār al-ḥarb to dār al-Islām.

3. A moderate position of scholars in the West defines dār al-Islām as any country in which a Muslim may freely practice his

3. Yohanann Friedmann, *Tolerance and Coercion in Islam: Interfaith Relations in the Muslim Tradition* (Cambridge: Cambridge University Press, 2003), p. 26.

4. The Muhajirun is a split-off of the Islamic Liberation Party (Hizb al-Tahrir al-Islami), which has as its main tenet the restoration of the caliphate.

5. MEMRI, *Special Dispatch Series* 435 (2002) quotes the leader of the movement, Sheikh Omar Bakri Muhammad.

religion. According to this interpretation, emigration from dār al-ḥarb is only an obligation if one fears not being able to practice Islam, or fears for his life or property because of being a Muslim. If a Muslim may practice Islam freely in his place of residence, despite its being secular or un-Islamic, he will be considered to be living in dār al-Islām. In this case, he is not obliged to emigrate; on the contrary, it may be better for him to remain to preach Islam where he is.[6]

4. A reformist definition of the category of dār al-ḥarb divides the world into dār al-Islām and the places where Muslims must spread Islam through preaching. In this case, dār al-Islām is any country in which there is a Muslim majority, even if the ruler does not completely abide by Islam.[7] Other reformists propose new categories, such as *dār al-'ahd* or *dār al-ṣulh* (countries with which there is a treaty or peace), *dār al-islaḥ*, or *dār al-ḍarura* (land of necessity), and *dār al-amān* (land of security).[8] Dār al-'ahd, it is reasoned, is by nature the prerogative of the rulers who are responsible for making the treaties; that most

6. Fatwā: Sheikh 'Atiyya Saqr, (11 October, 2002), www.islamonline.net/fatwā/english/FatwāDisplay.asp?hFatwāID = 51640. See also fatwās by Dr. Taha Jabir al-Alwani, president of the Graduate School of Islamic and Social Sciences in Virginia and President of the Fiqh Council of North America. Al-Alwani divides the world between dār al-Islām and *dār al-da'wa* and also supports renewal of ijtihad to deal with modern legal issues. A far-reaching extrapolation of this principle is that of the Italian sheikh Pallazi, who ruled that Israel cannot be viewed as dār al-ḥarb since the Muslims there may practice their religion and pray five times a day. A similar position was voiced by an Indian 'ulamā regarding India in the nineteenth century. Shamai Fishman, "Fiqh al-Aqaliyat."

7. Fatwā: Sheikh Faysal Mawlawi, "Fiqh al-Aqaliyat," 29 August 2002, www.islamonline.net/fatwā/english/FatwāDisplay.asp?hFatwāID = 72774.

8. Khaled Abou El Fadl, "Islamic Law and Muslim Minorities: The Juristic Discourse on Muslim Minorities from the Second/Eighth to the Eleventh/Seventeenth Centuries," *Islamic Law and Society*, 1, 2 (1994): 141–187; and Muhammad Khalid Masud, "Being Muslim in a Non-Muslim Polity: Three Alternate Models," *Journal of the Institute of Muslim Minority Affairs* 10, 1 (1989): 118–28.

Muslim countries are now members of the UN makes all the countries of the world dār al-ʿahd, not dār al-ḥarb.[9]

This same pragmatism is reflected in the Islamic classification of non-Muslims[10] into one of two basic categories: a follower of any polytheistic religion (*ahl al-shirk* or *mushrikūn*) or a member of one of the three recognized monotheistic religions of the Book, Judaism, Christianity, and Zoroastrianism (*ahl al-kitāb* or *kitābiyūn*). While Islam offers the former only acceptance of Islam, the latter may be a *dhimmi* who pays a head tax and is protected; a citizen of a country that has a treaty with the Muslim country (*muʿahad*), in which case he is protected; a citizen of a country of dār al-ḥarb that has no treaty with the Muslims, in which case he has no protection (*kāfir ḥarbi*); or a person protected by a writ of safe passage (*amān*) from a Muslim (either a government or, according to some, any Muslim).

Tempering this rigid classification is the verse in the Qur'an (2:256) that commands "no compulsion in religion." This principle became useful as Islam conquered lands whose people were no less polytheistic than the Arabs of the Arabian Peninsula but whose civilizations were robust and capable of withstanding Islam's allure. Thus, Zoroastrianism became a protected religion whose adherents were classified as "people of the Book," along with Jews and Christians. Later, in ninth- and tenth-century India, the Muslim conqueror ruled that the Hindu shrines were analogous to the churches and synagogues of Christians and Jews, thus absolving the Muslim rulers of India from the obligation of launching a never-ending jihād to convert the Hindus, a pragmatic approach that drew on the early rulings

9. Fatwā: Sheikh Faisal Mawlawi, "Does the U.S. Biased Policy Against Palestinians Make Her Dar Harb?" 8 September 2002, www.islamonline.net/fatwā/english/FatwāDisplay.asp?hFatwāID = 52392; mt.

10. The Islamic literary genre that treats this taxonomy is called *al-milāl wa al-nihal*. It analyzes the differences between the religions and the way that Islam should treat them.

of the Prophet in the Medina period. The first Islamic constitution, the Covenant of the Nation (*'ahd al-ummah*), regulated relations between Muslims and Jews, stipulating that they are "one Nation, separate from other Peoples," and that "the Jews of 'Awf are part of one nation with the believers. The Jews have their religion and the Muslims theirs." This precedent allowed Muslims to exercise relative tolerance toward the local polytheists who supported Islam. The close collaboration of Indian 'ulamā with the Indian national movement against the British was also legitimized by the Covenant of the Nation.[11]

Although Muslim liberals and reformists point to this stage in Muslim history (along with the later Golden Age in Andalusia) as proof of Islam's religious tolerance, the wider consensus is that such tolerance was superseded by the Prophet's later pronouncements. According to this interpretation, tolerance, then, grew out of the Muslims' "period of weakness," which forced them to compromise on spreading Islam. When that period ended, the Prophet was obliged to Islamize the peoples of Arabia, using as justification the forced conversions in medieval Christianity. Indeed, Islam, like Christianity, sees itself as destined to be the only faith in the entire world, and can interpret the conversion of others as part of an obligation to implement a manifest destiny. Furthermore, because the pagans are doomed to hell, converting them by force is an act of grace, saving them from eternal punishment.[12]

A Muslim, for his part, as mentioned earlier, is expected to live in dār al-Islām, and not to emigrate to dār al-ḥarb; if living in dār al-ḥarb, he is to emigrate. This duty emanates from the early emigration (*hijrah*) of Muslims from Mecca to avoid living among the kuf-

11. Yohanann Friedmann, "The Attitude of Jami'yyat-I 'Ulama Hind to the Indian National Movement and the Establishment of Pakistan," *Asian and African Studies* 7 (1971): 165.

12. Bonney, *Jihād*, p. 218; and Emmanuel Sivan, *Radical Islam: Medieval Theology and Modern Politics* (New Haven: Yale University Press, 1985), pp. 22–24. This view of Islam as a revolutionary religion was central to the thinking of the Pakistani Syed Abu'l A'la al-Maududi.

fār and to enable them to practice their new religion. But today the duty of emigration has another facet, with some scholars recommending it if it is in the context of jihād.[13] Their fatwās were behind a wave of mujāhidūn returning from the West to Afghanistan in early 2000.

Should a Muslim remain in a non-Muslim country, he is confronted with a complex set of social, economic, religious, and political dilemmas: May he befriend the local kuffār? May he participate in economic activities involving interest, which is forbidden in Islam? May he cooperate with believers of other religions on an equal level? May he stand for the national anthem or obey laws that may place him in a conflict with his commitment to the Muslim ummah or with Islamic precepts? May he serve in the military of a non-Muslim country? More generally, can the shari'ah, and particularly its prescribed punishments, be implemented in lieu of or in contradiction to the provisions of civil authorities? Recent fatwās raise the question of the legality of participating in democratic processes in dār al-ḥarb.

The problems of Muslims living in or passing through dār al-ḥarb or dār al-kufr were frequently solved in a pragmatic way by early Islamic scholars.[14] They continue to occupy scholars today— particularly those whose religious constituencies reside in the West. Those scholars have built up a large store of fatwās relating to Muslims in Western society which emphasize, among other things, the contradiction between participating in that society and allegiance to the ummah. Recently, a number of leading 'ulamā in the United States and Europe sanctioned such participation as permissible[15] or

13. Fatwā: Sheikh Muhammad Saleh al-Munajid, "Living in a Non-Muslim Country Seeking a Better Life," 23 February 2004, www.islamonline.net/fatwā/e nglish/FatwāDisplay.asp?hFatwāID = 110859.

14. El Fadl, *Islamic Law*, pp. 142–87. For example, some early scholars ruled that the *ḥudud* should not be implemented in dār al-ḥarb lest the Muslims join the kuffār to evade punishments.

15. These include the Islamic Summit in Detroit and the European Council of Fatwā, as well as the Egyptian Sheikh Ali Jad al-Haq, the Lebanese Sheikh Muham-

even as a duty, in order to "snatch away every bit of power they can" from the kuffār and to promote the Islamization of dār al-ḥarb.[16]

mad-Hussein Falallah, the Iraqi Sheikh Abdul-Karim Zaydan, and the Saudi Sheikh Muhammad-Saleh al-Munajed.

16. Amir Taheri, "The Islamic Urge to Vote," *New York Post*, 11 October 2004. This view is presented by Sheikh Yousuf al-Qaradawi, Sheikh Faisal al-Mawlawi, and Sheikh Makarem Shirazi.

CHAPTER 4

The Doctrine of Jihād

ISLAMIC jurisprudence notes various forms of military conflict: general war (*qital*), safeguarding the frontiers of dār al-Islām (*ribāṭ*), and jihād. Qital is generally forbidden between Muslims, being viewed as civil strife (*fitna*) and a grave sin, unless it is war against rebels and brigands. Ribāt is a more passive concept of homeland security. Jihād is, in essence, the Islamic form of sanctioned war—*bellum justum*.[1] Islamic law provides for war against apostates (contemporary Islamist oppositions frequently brand the rulers of Muslim states as such to justify total war against them), brigands, and rebels.[2] The law, however, does not exclude brigands from the fold of Islam or brand them as apostates.

Classical Islamic law, which took for granted that jihād was a military effort, focused on setting out the conditions under which it should be waged. Of the thirty-six instances in the Qur'an of the root j-h-d in various forms, only between ten and fourteen have a clear military connotation. The collections of the ḥadīth, however, contain hundreds of references to jihād, most of them in the context of military conflict. Be that as it may, "very little of the peaceful sense of j-h-d remained in Muslim culture, and the understanding of jihād

---

1. For an extensive discussion of the traditional law of war in Islam, see the classic book Khadduri, *War and Peace*.

2. Abou El Fadl, *Rebellion*, p. 32.

as war became predominant . . . [T]he warlike meaning of jihād thus predominates, to the extent that q-t-l ('kill') was sometimes glossed by j-h-d."[3]

The frequent juxtaposition in Islamic sources of jihād and martyr-dom leaves little doubt that the early Muslims saw jihād first and foremost as military confrontation with the enemies of the ummah, particularly in "jihād on the path of Allah" (fi sabīl Allah), widely interpreted as a strictly military jihād. In fact, jihād is one of the most laudable deeds that a Muslim may perform; both the Qur'an and hadīth are replete with examples of the high esteem in which Islam holds the mujāhid and of the rewards he receives in paradise after his death. The Prophet, in an effort to overcome the natural reservations of people about war, pointed out the inadequacy of the human conscience with regard to matters of jihād and the danger of leaving the question of participation to the discretion of the individ-ual, abstract morality, or politics. He cautioned that "fighting is or-dered for you even though you dislike it and it may be that you dislike a thing that is good for you and like a thing that is bad for you. Allah knows but you do not know" (Qu'ran 2:216).

Jihād's centrality in Islam is as old as Islam itself. The original jihād consisted of the military struggle against the polytheists of the Arabian Peninsula, with the goal of converting them to Islam. Within the boundaries of the Arabian homeland, no polytheism—and eventually no other monotheistic religion—could be tolerated. Although participating in jihād was a great deed in the eyes of early Islam, it remained a means to the end of the promulgation of Islam. As the Islamic state stabilized under the caliphs and polytheism dis-appeared from dār al-Islām, jihād became a recommended act for most Muslims, and a duty when ordered by the caliph against exter-nal infidels. Most early mujtāhidun were cautious about making jihād an overall duty—even against polytheists if they did not initiate

3. Ella Landau-Tasseron, "Jihād," in *Encyclopedia of the Qur'an*, Jane McAuliff, ed. (Leiden, England: Brill Academic Publishers, 2003).

the hostilities—and preferred to leave it to the discretion of the caliph. As a causus belli for jihād, heresy was a necessary condition, but it had to be augmented by political circumstances.

After the death of the Prophet, however, a minority group, known by their opponents as Kharijites (*Khawarij*), or "secessionists," saw jihād as a pillar of Islam. Accusing other Muslims of apostasy, they waged jihād against them. Although the Kharijites were defeated, and reviled in Muslim history, they represent a tendency that has appeared time and again over the centuries, a tendency to resuscitate the historic dawn of Islam—the pristine era of the ummah, during which God bestowed on the Muslims his grace, success, and particularly political and military predominance—by re-creating the events of the time and emulating the behavior of the Prophet. Early twentieth-century Islamic fundamentalism restored jihād to the center of Islamic thought. Hassan al-Banna, founder of the Muslim Brotherhood, argued that jihād is an obligation, as much as any of the other five pillars of Islam, for every Muslim.[4] The parallel between the Kharijites and contemporary Islamic radicals has been noted by scholars of Islam.[5] One of the harsher condemnations that moderate and establishment 'ulamā hurl at radicals today is that they are modern-day Kharijites.

The nonbelligerent definitions of jihād—as efforts on the spiritual, social, and educational levels to spread the word of the Prophet and belief in Islam—are, of course, legitimate. Such interpretations appeared early in the development of Islam. Their relative absence from Islamic legal literature may be accounted for by the fact that, unlike the military jihād, they did not pose much of a legal dilemma.

4. Richard P. Mitchell, *The Society of the Muslim Brotherhood* (Oxford: Oxford University Press, 1969), p. 207. The five pillars of Islam are Shahadah (the declaration of faith that there is no God but Allah and Muhammad is his Prophet), Salat (prayer), Sawm (fasting on the Ramadan), Haj (pilgrimage to Mecca), and Zakat (charity).

5. Johannes J.G. Jansen, "The Early Islamic Movement of the Kharidjites and Modern Moslem Extremism: Similarities and Differences," *Orient* 27, 1 (1986).

One explanation for the option of substituting nonmilitary acts for physical jihād may be that jihād had been institutionalized through a standing army. Once it had become unnecessary for every able-bodied Muslim to wage jihād, most of the population became exempt from military service. The "duty" of jihād and its merits, though, were not abolished: civil expressions of jihād became alternatives to this important duty.[6]

Contemporary definitions of jihād range from an exclusively military undertaking against the kuffār to the struggles of a human being with the evil inclinations of his own soul. The Saudi sheikh 'Abd al-'Aziz ibn Baz (head of the High 'Ulamā Council and the Islamic World League) defined thirteen different forms of jihād, ranging from jihād with one's soul (*jihād al-nefs*)—that is, a person going into battle (not to be confused with the *jihād bil-nafs*, struggle against one's own soul, that is, the evil inclination)—to jihād with one's wealth, to jihād with one's tongue, or proselytizing.[7] Ibn Baz's taxonomy is accepted by most non-radical and establishment 'ulamā, who acknowledge the duty of jihād in Islam but find legal justifications in traditional jurisprudence to suspend it. Those scholars tend to define jihād as a struggle against heresy in general, not necessarily a military struggle against nonbelievers. They emphasize, when applicable and politically expedient (for example, in the case of the West but not in the case of Israel), the spiritual interpretation of jihād and its implementation, mainly through proselytizing, while playing down its military connotations.

Several arguments support this non-militaristic interpretation of jihād. First, a verse in the Qur'an (9:73) calls to "strive against the disbelievers and the hypocrites." Because the hypocrites (*munāfiqun*) are Muslims, and a Muslim cannot wage a military jihād against an-

6. I owe this historic interpretation to Prof. Ella Landau-Tasseron of the Hebrew University of Jerusalem.

7. *Fatawa al-Shaykh Ibn Baz* (The fatwās of Sheikh Ibn Baz) 7/334, 335. See also Muhammad ibn Ahmad al-Salam, 39 *Wasilah li-khidmat al-jihād wal-musharikah fihi* (39 ways to serve the jihād and to participate in it) (n.p.: 1424 (hijri), 2003).

other Muslim, the verse is construed to mean that the striving cannot be in the form of war.[8] Second, the only way to spread Islam in the time of the Prophet was through the sword. Today, however, there are many other ways to do so: through mass media, the Internet, and so forth. Some argue that the concept of jihād was relevant in the seventh century and is not relevant in the modern world, but such an argument may contradict the timelessness of the Prophet's messages. Third, some scholars maintain that Muslims are relatively weak and that harm will come to the Muslim ummah if it wages a military jihād against the rest of the world.

One modernist (and to some extent, mystic Sufi) definition uses a linguistic analysis of the word *jihād* (*jahada,* to strive) to divest it of its military connotations.[9] According to this definition, jihād is the "self-exertion" of a Muslim to discipline his soul, improve his faith, and struggle against his own evil inclinations. Supporting this definition is a ḥadīth in which the Prophet greeted soldiers on their return from war and told them that they had now returned from the "small jihād" (war) to the "great jihād," (against one's own evil inclinations). This interpretation is not relevant to a discussion of the laws of jihād, for once it has been determined that jihād is not a military struggle, the other issues of jus in bello do not apply. Of interest, however, is that the "great jihād" presupposes the "small jihād" and that radical sheikhs have endeavored to discredit that ḥadīth altogether, relying, among other things, on the assertion of Sheikh Ibn Taymiya that it is spurious.[10]

The radical definition, in contrast, views jihād exclusively as a military conflict between the Muslims and the kuffār. This understand-

8. Fatwā: Sheikh Muhammad 'Ali Al-Hanooti, "Levels of Jihād," 23 April 2002, www.islamonline.net/fatwā/english/FatwāDisplay.asp?hFatwāID = 19944.

9. This is a rather specious argument. In all occurrences of the concept in traditional Islamic texts—and more significantly, the accepted meaning for the great majority of modern Muslims—the term means "a divinely ordained war."

10. *Nida'ul Islam Magazine* 26 (April–May 1999), www.islam.org.au; and Bonney, *Jihād,* p. 117.

ing, which is deeply embedded in orthodox Islamic interpretations and traditions, relies on a number of considerations. First, it appeals to the duty to emulate the Prophet and his Companions: the Prophet strove in military jihād most of his later life, and it behooves a Muslim to imitate this behavior. Second, it invokes the explicit statements in the Qur'an (2:216): "Fighting is enjoined on you and it is an object of dislike to you and there may be that you dislike a thing and it is good for you. Allah knows best . . ." and Qur'an (8:39): "And fight them until there is no more dissent and the religion will be for Allah alone." These verses are interpreted as clear commands to conduct a jihād whenever possible. Third, it seeks to refute the authenticity of the ḥadīth on the lesser jihād and the greater jihād.[11]

Furthermore, in the radical view, a military jihād—and, of course, martyrdom—has both spiritual and temporal value, "impl[ying] all kinds of worship, both in its inner and outer forms. More than any other act it implies love and devotion for Allah, trust in Him, the surrender of one's life and property to Him, patience, asceticism, remembrance of Allah, and all kinds of other acts [of worship]. And the individual or community that participates in it finds itself between two blissful outcomes: victory and triumph or martyrdom and Paradise."[12] A military jihād allows Muslim forces to retreat only if their numerical strength is less than half that of the enemy or, less pragmatically, in the face of a tenfold enemy superiority.

Islamic legal sources distinguish between two types of military jihād according to the conditions that initiate them and the nature of the enemy. The "offensive jihād" or "initiated jihād" (*jihād al-talab waal-ibtida*) is a "collective duty" (*farḍ kiffāya*) of the Muslim community to pursue the infidels into their own lands, call on them to accept Islam, and fight them if they refuse to do so. It can only be

---

11. "Ruling on Physical Jihād," www.islam-qa.com, fatwā no. 34830.

12. Ibn Taymiyyah, *Al-Siyasah al-shar'iyyah fi Islah al-ra'i wa al-ra'iyya* (The Shari'ah Policy Regarding the Reform of the Ruler and His Flock) (Beirut: Dār al-Fikr al-Ḥadth).

implemented by an Islamic ruler (the caliph)—who appoints believers to guard the borders and sends out an army at least once a year. If the caliph has appointed specific Muslims to perform this duty, it is not incumbent on the rest of the Muslim community. The "defensive jihād" (*jihād al-difā*) is an "individual duty" (*farḍ 'ain*) by which all Muslims must defend Muslim lands when the infidels are prepared to attack, when they attack and occupy them, and when Muslims face infidels on the battlefield. Although an individual rather than a collective duty, it is no less a religious imperative than the other five pillars of Islam. A Muslim who does not perform it will not inherit Paradise.

Few modern sheikhs claim that there is a current collective duty on Muslims to wage an offensive jihād. Such a jihād has been deferred to a time when Muslims can extricate themselves from a "period of weakness," pending the revival of a Muslim caliphate. Because jihād for spreading Islam is the obligation of the Islamic state, it can only be performed under the command of the caliph or a "commander of the faithful." In the absence of those conditions, the duty is in abeyance. For some Sunni 'ulamā, however, the suspension of jihād leads them to conclude that it is the duty of Muslims to restore the Islamic state and to elect a caliph, who will in turn restore the offensive collective jihād. [13] The duty of jihād under a caliphate is of particular significance, since the restoration of the caliphate is one of the primary goals of the jihādist movement today (al-Qa'ida and its offshoots such as Abu Mus'ab al-Zarqawi in Iraq). According to this ideology, once a caliphate exists, it is the foremost duty of the caliph to ensure the purity of Islam within the borders of the caliphate. The immediate meaning is that there can be no tolerance toward heterodox Muslims such as Shiites. This principle is em-

13. Omar Bakri Muhammad, quoted in "Islamist Leader in London: No Universal Jihād as Long as There Is No Caliphate" *MEMRI, Special Dispatch Series* 435 (2002). The Hizb al-Tahrir and Muhajerun movements are the best examples of this thinking.

ployed in the present campaign of Zarqawi against the Shiites of Iraq.

Even under a caliphate, some scholars list three additional prerequisites for jihād: First, Muslims must not embark on jihād unless they have a strong base and are powerful; the Prophet himself did not embark on jihād while he was weak, waiting until he became strong and had enough supporters and a land from which to depart and to which to return. Second, before engaging the kuffār in battle, the Muslims must call on them to accept Islam and the offer must be rejected. And third, the jihād must be in line with Muslims' general interests (*maslahah*), and should not cause harm to them or to the cause of spreading Islam. (The last is a catchall that allows great latitude in forgoing jihād.)

Whereas Sunni Islam leaves room for renewing the offensive jihād if and when the Muslims choose a caliph, traditional Shiite Islam defers it to an apocalyptic era when the Hidden Imām (the twelfth Imām, who is in occultation (*ghayba*) and will appear at the end of days as the Mahdī) will take revenge on the enemies of Allah and bring order and justice to the world.[14] Shiite tradition does not allow for an Imām substitute, though some scholars hold that certain powers of the Imām may be delegated during his occultation. Like the Sunni defensive jihād, the Shiite concept allows for jihād for "defense of the ummah," a term that may include defense against attacks or occupation of Muslim lands by non-Muslims; protecting Muslim property, freedom, and dignity; suppressing rebellion by non-Muslims (*dhimmi*); supporting rebellion against despotism; or even punishing Muslims guilty of corruption (*fasād*) or destruction (*hirābah*). In such cases, determining the duty of jihād and leading the Muslims in it is up to the highest scholars (mujtāhidūn). The Shiite view of jihād against other Muslims was manifest in the Iranian attitude toward Iraq under Saddam Hussein. When war broke out between Iran and Iraq in 1980, the Iranian regime could have

14. Assaf Moghadam, "The Shi'i Perception of Jihād," *AlNakhlah* (Fall 2003): 3.

declared it a matter of national defense. Instead, Ayatollah Khomeini declared it a jihād and an individual duty. The Farsi terminology used to describe the war left no doubt regarding its sacredness— "holy defense" or "jihād for the cause of God."[15]

Religious categorizations of Saddam Hussein were also important to Iran in justifying the war. Saddam was branded *zalim* (oppressor), *fasiq* (sinner), *fasid* (causer of corruption, *fasād*) *mushrik* (polytheist, pagan), *mulhid* (deviator), *mustakbir* (pretender to superior or divine status, arrogant), *baghī* (a Muslim who rebels against God or his Imām and, hence in Shiite theology, a heretic), *taghūt* (a ruler who defies God), and *kāfir* (infidel). These epithets were not mere rhetoric against the nation's arch-enemy; each of them implies a religious duty to wage jihād. Almost all of them entail continuing the jihād until the enemy is eliminated or repents, which means that Iran would be required to "fight them until there is no dissent" (Qur'an II:193, VIII:39), that is, to continue until victory.[16] Indeed, Khomeini's own statements reflected his religious reasoning and absolute authority and seemed to indicate that the war would go on as long as he lived.[17] Negotiation and peace with such a kāfir was forbidden by Islam.[18]

The contemporary doctrine of jihād is permeated by apocalyptical and eschatological ideas and fueled by texts and concepts that had fallen into desuetude and then been recycled.[19] Eschatological be-

15. Saskia Gieling, *Religion and War in Revolutionary Iran* (London: Tauris, 1999), pp. 44–50.

16. Ibid., pp. 80–94.

17. As mentioned above, a Marja' Taqlīd is to be followed by his Muqallidun only as long as he lives. A Shiite Muslim cannot be a Muqallid of a dead Marja'. Ostensibly, this mechanism can open the door for decisions that create a religious conundrum left by a dead leader. Insofar as Khomeini is concerned, however, the revolutionary regime has set new standards by declaring that no one may abrogate the fatwās issued by Khomeini. The most blatant example is that of the fatwā regarding Salman Rushdie.

18. Gieling, p. 165.

19. Reuven Paz, "Global Jihād and the Sense of Crisis: al-Qa'idah's Other Front," *Prism Series of Global Jihād*, 1, 4 (2003).

liefs had played a role in Islamic revivalism as far back as the move-ment of the Mahdī in Sudan and the November 1979 attack on the great mosque in Mecca by Juhaiman al-'Utaibi and the self-styled Mahdī Muhammad bin 'Abdallah al-Qahtani.[20] Although most scholars tend to restrict their fatwās to practical instructions regard-ing the duties of jihād, some recent ones shed light on the eschato-logical elements, signs related in hadīths by the Prophet regarding the coming of the Last Day and linking them to contemporary events. For example, Sheikh Yousuf Qaradawi saw that "the signs of salvation are absolute, numerous, and as plain as day, indicating that the future belongs to Islam and that Allah's religion will defeat all other religions . . . the conquest of Rome and the spread of Islam till it includes all that is in night and day . . . are prelude to the return of the Caliphate."[21] The West, the United States, and Israel are lik-ened to the ancient tribes of 'Ad and Thamud, which, according to the Qur'an, rejected the message of Muhammad and were therefore annihilated, or to the generation of Noah, which Allah decreed to be drowned. Before the September 11 attacks, the United States was likened to ancient Egypt, to which Allah sent a series of plagues, fi-nally drowning Pharaoh's troops in the sea.[22]

Other eschatological references are found in fatwās that refer to the Soviet defeat in Afghanistan (which, along with the subsequent fall of the Soviet Union, marked the renewal of the jihād against the infidel world at large and the apocalyptic war between Islam and her-esy that will result in Islam's rule over the world), the U.S. campaigns against Afghanistan and Iraq, and the Palestinian Intifada. Refer-

20. M.H. Ansari, *The Islamic Boomerang in Saudi Arabia: The Cost of Delayed Reforms* (New Delhi: ORF Samskriti, 2004), pp. 9–11.

21. Fatwā: Yousuf Qaradawi, *"Mubasharat fi intisar al-Islam"* (Portents for the victory of Islam), 1 April 2002, www.islamonline.net/fatwā/arabic/FatwāDisplay .asp?hFatwāID = 2042.

22. Fatwā: Sheikh al-Khudheir, 21 September 2001, quoted in *MEMRI, Special Report* 25 (2004), http://memri.org/bin/articles.cgi?Page = archives&Area = sr&ID = SR2504# ...edn12; and http://saaid.net/Warathah/khudier/k5.htm.

ences to eschatological events are also mustered to support jihād as the means of hastening the coming of the Last Day. Here the Israeli-Arab conflict is presented as fulfilling a widely quoted ḥadīth, according to which, "The (last) hour will not come until the Muslims fight the Jews and kill them. A Jew will hide behind a rock or a tree, and the rock or tree will call upon the Muslim: 'O Muslim, O Slave of Allah! There is a Jew behind me, come and kill him.'"[23]

---

23. Sahih Muslim *Hadith*, Book 41, no. 6985.

CHAPTER 5

The Defensive Jihād, an Individual Duty

I F jihād is by definition a military conflict, the question remains whether a specific conflict warrants being defined as a jihād. One must also ask whether participation is an individual duty or only a recommended act? Or is it a duty for some and recommended for others? Is it a sin to refrain from participation of any sort in a jihād?

Most contemporary fatwās on jihād agree that it becomes an individual duty, incumbent on all sane and healthy adult Muslim males who have reached the age of puberty, under several specific circumstances. First, jihād becomes a duty if the imam calls on an individual to fight after having deemed the situation a legitimate jihād. Then, the command of the ruler becomes an individual religious duty that may not be shirked. Jihād also becomes a duty if the armies of Muslims and kuffār approach each other. A Muslim is not permitted to flee from battle, and it is his individual duty to fight. The reluctance to retreat stems from the belief that jihād is an act of faith in Allah. In fighting a weaker or equal enemy, the Muslim relies on his own strength, not on Allah's, whereas by entering the fray against all odds, the mujāhid proves his utter faith in Allah and will be rewarded accordingly. Finally, jihād becomes a duty when a country in which Muslims live is attacked by kuffār (in which case the jihād is defensive, by definition) or when kuffār take a group of Muslims prisoner.[1]

Under these circumstances, jihād becomes an individual duty "like prayer and fasting during the month of Ramadan."[2] Because jihād as an individual obligation is a fundamental duty (shirking it may condemn a Muslim to hell), it is not subject to many pragmatic considerations. The very act of defying a superior military force in battle expresses the acceptance of the yoke of Allah and submission to his will. The Qur'an is ambivalent on the issue of retreating in the face of superior enemy forces. At first it forbids it entirely (except tactical retreats), then later allows retreat in the face of a tenfold superiority of the enemy and, ultimately, it allows retreat in the face of a two-to-one superiority.

Contemporary fatwās tend to allow retreat in the face of the enemy in two situations: bringing reinforcements or joining a group that is in danger, as long as there is no risk to one's own group.[3]

A number of seminal tracts and fatwās by various radical scholars and leaders argue in favor of an individual duty of defensive jihād. An early example of such a fatwā was that of Egyptian jihād leader Abd al-Salam Farag, whose small 1988 tract, aptly entitled "Jihād: The Forsaken Duty" (*al-jihād—al-farīḍa al-ghayba*) inspired generations of radicals. In it Farag argued, like the seventh-century kharijites before him, that jihād is a duty for every Muslim no less than the obligatory five pillars that Muslims are obligated to perform.[4]

The argument for the existence of a defensive jihād derives from

1. 'Abdallah 'Azzam, *'Al-difa' an ard al-Muslimin aham furūḍ al-'ayn* (The defense of the lands of the Muslims: The most important of the individual duties) (Jedda: Dar al-Mujtama', 1987), p. 20.

2. Ibid.

3. Fatwā: Sheikh Muhammad Saleh Al-Munajjid, "Jihād: Not Only Fighting," 12 April, 2003, Islam Online, www.islamonline.net/fatwā/english/FatwaDisplay. asp?hFatwaID=96325. See also Muhammad 'Ayyash Al-Kubeisi, "Min Fiqh al-Muqawma" (On the law of resistance), *Al-Sabil* (Jordan), 1 March 2005.

4. R. Hrair Dekmejian, *Islam in Revolution: Fundamentalism in the Arab World* (New York: Syracuse University Press, 1995), pp. 94–95.

the Islamic identity of Muslim lands. Much as individual Muslims cannot convert (or even revert) to any other faith (hence capital punishment for apostates such as Salman Rushdie), any land once under the sway of Islamic law may not be controlled by any other law. Were such a thing to happen, it is the "individual duty" of all Muslims in the land to fight a jihād to liberate it. If they do not succeed, any Muslim within a certain perimeter of that land must join the jihād. This duty spreads to Muslims farther and farther away until the Muslim land has been liberated. Hence, the very existence of a defensive jihād entails an individual duty to take up arms, at least for the Muslims living in the threatened country.

In Islamic law there is no statute of limitations on usurpation and "conversion" of lands belonging to dār al-Islām—the longer the occupation of a given land, the greater the duty of the Muslims to liberate it. Thus, "Spain had been a Muslim territory for more than eight hundred years before it was captured by the Christians. They [the Christians] literally and practically wiped out the whole Muslim population. And now it is our duty to restore Muslim rule to this land of ours. The whole of India, including Kashmir, Hyderabad, Assam, Nepal, Burma, Behar, and Junagadh, was once a Muslim territory. But we lost this vast territory, and it fell into the hands of the disbelievers simply because we abandoned jihād. And Palestine, as is well-known, is currently under the occupation of the Jews. Even our First Qibla, Bayt-al-Muqaddas, is under their illegal possession."[5] Thus a Muslim may not excuse himself from jihād just because the conditions for it do not exist in his country. Rather, he is expected to seek out the jihād and to participate in it. This has become one of the ideological building blocks of the internationalization of jihād struggles in Afghanistan, Bosnia, and, lately, Iraq.

The harbinger of the modern global jihād doctrine was the Jordanian-Palestinian Sheikh Abdallah 'Azzam (1941–1989), who encour-

---

5. "Jihād ul-Kuffār wal-Munāfiqīn (Jihad against the infidels and the hypocrites)," unsigned text.

aged the solidarity of the believers and prohibited reliance on nonbelievers (though the mujāhidūn in Afghanistan pragmatically realized that international politics makes strange bedfellows). Sheikh 'Azzam's fatwās, which are still widely quoted in the responses of today's radical 'ulamā, call for continuous jihād "until all of Mankind worships Allah." He did not, however, stop at determining jihād as the primary means for achieving Allah's rule; jihād became a moral goal in itself. In his preaching and writing he reiterated, "A few moments spent in jihād in the Path of Allah is worth more than seventy years spent in praying at home." Waging jihād was, for 'Azzam and his followers, a way to imitate the Prophet and his Companions by reenacting the events of the seventh century—belief, emigration from infidel society (the hijrah of the Prophet from Mecca), and finally jihād for spreading Islam. The implicit goal, in Sheikh 'Azzam's view, was reestablishing the caliphate through jihād (ultimately offensive jihād) until Islam holds sway over the world.

In the wake of the Soviet invasion of Afghanistan in 1979, 'Abdallah 'Azzam issued the fatwā "Defense of the Muslim Lands." This fatwā, supported by Saudi Arabia's Grand Mufti, 'Abd al-'Aziz Bin Baz, ruled that both the Afghan and the Palestinian struggles were jihāds in which killing kuffār was a duty for all Muslims:

> The 'ulamā of the four schools of jurisprudence, the compilers of the ḥadīth and the commentators of the Qur'an all agree that . . . jihād becomes an individual obligation for the Muslims of the land that the kuffār have attacked and for the Muslims close by, where the children will march forth without the permission of the parents, the wife without the permission of her husband, and the debtor without the permission of the creditor. And, if the Muslims of this land cannot expel the kuffār because of lack of forces, because they slacken, are indolent, or simply do not act, then the individual obligation spreads in the shape of a circle from the nearest to the next nearest. If they too slacken or there is again a shortage of manpower, then it is upon the people behind them, and on the people behind them, to march for-

ward. This process continues until it becomes an individual obligation [for all Muslims in the world].

If the Muslims do not fulfill this obligation it is a great sin:

> The sin is on the necks of all the Muslims as long as even a hand span of land is in the hands of the kuffār. The sin is measured according to one's authority or capabilities; therefore the sin for the 'ulamā, the leaders, and the *Da'i* [caller to Islam], who are well known in their communities, is greater than for the ordinary civilian. The sin upon this present generation—for advancing toward Afghanistan, Palestine, Kashmir, Lebanon, Chad, Eritrea, etc.—is greater than the sin inherited from the loss of these lands, which have previously fallen into the possession of the kuffār.[6]

'Azzam himself, although of Palestinian-Jordanian origin, ruled that the jihād in Afghanistan takes precedence over the jihād in Palestine. The arena for the performance of the duty of jihād was, in his eyes, not to be chosen on the basis of emotion but according to a political-military calculus:

> It is our opinion that we should begin with Afghanistan before Palestine, not because Afghanistan is more important than Palestine—not at all—for Palestine is the foremost Islamic problem. Indeed, it is the heart of the Islamic world, and it is a blessed land, but there are some pressing reasons that make Afghanistan the [preferable] starting point. (1) The battles in Afghanistan are still raging and have reached a level of intensity, the likes of which have not been witnessed in the mountain ranges of Hindu Kush, or in recent Islamic history. (2) The raising of the Islamic flag in Afghanistan is clear, and the aim is clear: "To make Allah's words uppermost."[7]

6. 'Abdallah 'Azzam, *Al-difa' an Ard al-Muslimin*, p. 29.
7. Ibid., p. 31

Abdallah 'Azzam also rejected the idea that a jihād cannot be conducted in the absence of an accepted leader to whom the mujāhidūn can give their oath of fealty (ba'ya), claiming that no formal Commander of the Believers was necessary because the jihād is an individual duty.

The revolutionary underlying concept, however, was not confined to the Afghani theatre. Taking into account the number of Muslim lands under occupation and the length of those occupations, it became an individual duty for all Muslims to join the jihād, known as the "general call to arms or levy."[8] This doctrine was adopted by those "Arab Afghans," including Osama bin Laden, who came to fight alongside the Afghani mujāhidūn. The Afghani crucible also had far-reaching effects outside Afghanistan and the Arab world. The participation of Muslims from the former Soviet Union and from Southeast Asia (the Philippines, Malaysia, and Indonesia) spurred the migration of the idea of jihād to those countries, which was reinforced by Saudi Wahhabi missionaries, the Iranian export of Islam, and the cross-pollination of ideas in the information era. Fatwās issued in Afghanistan became guidelines for jihād in completely different environments.

Many fatwās on jihād went far beyond obliging individual Muslims to participate, branding as sinners Muslim leaders, both religious and political, who did not actively take part. Abdallah 'Azzam's ideological successors, including bin Laden, took this one step further, accusing such leaders of heresy—not only for not enforcing shari'ah generally, but for being derelict in the duty of jihād.

Another step in jihād's internationalization can be seen in the absence of references in recent fatwās to the theater in which jihād takes place or the kuffār against whom it is waged. This doctrine ascribes to jihād a value on its own, only when necessary or when the opportunity presents itself, leading to the conclusion that a Muslim

---

8. *Al-nafir al-'aām*, based on Qur'an (9:41): "March forth whether you are light or heavy and strive hard with your wealth and your lives."

must strive to participate. No Muslim who takes part in jihād "will be touched by hellfire and conversely, he who dies without having fought in jihād or attempting to do so will die a hypocrite [*munāfiq*]" (the designation of those who claimed to be Muslims but betrayed the Prophet and therefore are condemned to the lowest level of hell).⁹ The Qur'an verses supporting this doctrine are the Verses of the Sword (9:5, 9:36); Surat al-Anfal (Chapter 8: The Spoils of War); Surat al-Qital (Chapter 47: The Battle also known as Surat Muhammad); and Surat al-Fath (Chapter 48: The Victory). Because the majority of the proponents of jihād are followers of the Hanbali School, they do not raise the question of the possible abrogation of any of these verses by later, more pacific, verses.

The Afghanistan veterans who returned to their various homes brought with them a new justification for jihād. For many of them, the analogy between the Soviet occupation of Afghanistan that warranted jihād as an individual duty and the situation in their own lands was clear. Thus, fatwās modeled after those of 'Abdallah 'Azzam began to appear in other parts of the Muslim world. The dominant legal authority for them remained, however, that of the heartland of Islam: the Arab world in general and Saudi Arabia in particular. The leader of the Indonesian Laskar Jihād organization claimed that he had received seven fatwās—six from Saudi Arabia and one from Yemen—justifying jihād as an individual duty to defend against attacks by Christians. The Indonesian organization did not find, or did not feel the need to find, a local mufti to support those fatwās.¹⁰

In the wake of the Iraqi invasion of Kuwait and Operation Desert Storm, the same circles saw an analogy between the Afghani and the Iraqi cases. Although there was little love lost between the jihād movement and the secular Baathist regime of Saddam Hussein, both

---

9. Fatwā: Sheikh 'Abd al-'Aziz ibn Baz, "Ḥadīths on the Merits of Jihād," n.d., www.islamonline.net/fatwā/english/FatwāDisplay.asp?hFatwāID = 18245.

10. Eliraz, *Islam in Indonesia*, p. 30.

saw the U.S. attack on Iraq as part of a grand design to subjugate the Muslim nation, to appropriate its wealth, and to lead its peoples away from the faith of Mohammad.

The fatwā issued by the World Islamic Front for Jihād against the Jews and the Crusaders, headed by Osama bin Laden, extended this principle to justify war against the United States.[11] It argues that the United States has been occupying the lands of Islam in the holiest of places, the Arabian Peninsula, plundering its riches, dictating to its rulers, and turning its bases into a spearhead through which to fight the neighboring Muslim peoples. Thus it is incumbent on each Muslim to follow the Qur'an and "fight the pagans all together as they fight you all together . . . fight them until there is not corruption (fasād) or oppression." The fatwā also justifies the original offensive jihād: "Fight and slay the pagans wherever you find them, seize them and beleaguer them, and lie in wait for them in every stratagem" (Qur'an 9:5). And a hadīth quotes the Prophet as saying, "I have been sent with the sword between my hands to ensure that no one save Allah is worshipped."[12]

The same logic was applied in the wake of September 11 and the American attacks on Afghanistan and later on Iraq. Because those attacks were seen as aiming to subjugate the Islamic ummah and even to attack Islam itself, jihād becomes an individual duty for all Muslims.[13]

The existence of a defensive jihād also raises the problem of the participation of women and minors. Rulings on women participating in battle (or in suicide attacks) largely focus on questions of modesty and the control over them of men—fathers and brothers if they are not married, husbands if they are married, and sons or other kin if they are widowed.[14] The growing use of female suicide bombers by

11. "Fatwā of the World Islamic Front," *Al-Quds al-Arabi*, 23 February 1998.

12. Ibid.

13. Fatwā: Islamic Research Academy, *Al-Azhar* (Egypt), 11 March 2003, on the possibility of an attack on Iraq.

14. Fatwā: Sheikh Yousuf Qaradawi, "Palestinian Women Carrying Out Martyr Operations," 22 March 2004, http://islamonline.net/fatwāaplication/english/display.

Palestinian and Chechnyan jihād movements has brought this issue to the fore.

Two conflicting attitudes prevail. One, the traditionalist approach, recognizes a woman's right to participate in a defensive jihād but recommends that she do so in a way that poses no risk or danger to her honor. This involves non-combat roles such as nursing the wounded, preparing food, carrying weapons, and bringing water to the fighters, or providing the army with money, propagating the just cause of Muslim wars through modern technology, and so on. According to this approach, even a voluntary Haj to Mecca is considered participation in the jihād.[15]

In the case of a defensive jihād, a modern radical approach relies on traditions according to which a woman may go into battle without obtaining her husband's consent, a child without his parents' consent, and a slave without his master's consent.[16] In such cases a woman does not need a chaperone and may even expose her hair (remove the veil) because she does so not in order to show off her beauty but to carry out the operation.[17]

The issue of minors' participating in jihād was also debated in early Islamic jurisprudence and has now become relevant in light of the use of minors in suicide attacks (particularly by Palestinian Is-

---

asp?hFatwaID = 68511. Issued in response to the question of "women carrying out martyr operations. Fulfilling this mission may demand that they travel alone, without a *mahram* (escort from her family), and they may need to take off their hijab, which may expose part of their *'awrah* (parts of the body which are supposed to be covered)."

15. Fatwā: Sheikh Sayed Sabiq, "Jihād: When and Upon Whom?" 7 April 2002, www.islamonline.net/fatwā/english/FatwāDisplay.asp?hFatwaID = 18232; and Dr. 'Abdel-Fattaah Idrees, "Muslim Women Participating in Jihād," 23 August 2002.

16. "What Role Can Sisters Play in Jihād?" *Islam Awakening*, Azzam Publications, Article 623, www.as-sahwah.com/viewarticle.php?articleID = 623&.

17. Sheikh Yusuf bin Saleh al-'Airi, *"Dur al-nissā' fi jihād al-aāda'"* (The role of women in the jihād against the enemy), *Salsilat al-buhuth wa-aldirasat al-shar;iya* no. 7. *Markaz al buḥuth wa-aldirasāt al-shari'ya*, n.d. Fatwā: Sheikh Yousuf Qaradawi, "Palestinian Women Carrying Out Martyr Operations," 22 March 2004, islamonline.net/fatwāaplication/english/display.asp?hFatwaID = 68511.

lamic organizations). One approach leans on traditions according to which the Prophet forbade minors—or even adults whose parents or children were totally dependent on them—to participate in jihād.[18]

The modern debate among Islamic scholars regarding the right or obligation of women and minors to participate in jihād touches on the open nerves of modern Islamic society. Two of the main complaints against the infiltration of western values into Islamic society involve the demand for gender equality and the disruption of the traditional authority of elders over the young. Blanket dispensation for individual initiatives of women and minors undercuts the very authority in whose name the scholars claim to speak. It is, therefore, not remarkable that decisions by the more "conservative" or "orthodox" organizations to refrain from or limit the use of women and children under thirteen in suicide bombings have encountered little criticism even from radical circles.

18. Fatwās: Sheikh Sayyed Sabiq, "Jihād: When and Upon Whom?" 7 April 2002, www.islamonline.net/fatwā/english/FatwāDisplay.asp?hFatwāID = 18232. It may be assumed that the traditional approach had its rationale in the burden that would fall on the community to maintain the survivors of the young shahīd. This is reminiscent of the biblical rules for participation in war: "What man has betrothed a wife and not taken her? Let him return to his house lest he die in battle" (Deuteronomy 20:5–8).

CHAPTER 6

Rules of Engagement

The Targets

ONE of the questions most relevant to the justification of terrorism is how to define a legitimate target. Fatwās deal with this by identifying three main categories: who should be killed, who may be saved (by discretion), and who must be spared.

Classic Islamic law of jihād paid considerable attention to these questions. It distinguished between types of kuffār: idolaters within the Arabian peninsula who must accept Islam or be put to death, and Jews, Christians, and Zoroastrians (the People of the Book —*ahl al-kitab*) who may pay the head tax and live under the protection of the Muslims as *dhimmi* (protected persons or communities). Dhimmi status only applies to non-Muslims who are involved when a jihād takes place in dār al-Islām. When the fighting takes place in dār al-ḥarb (or even a Muslim country that is occupied and has, therefore, become dār al-ḥarb), Jews, Christians, and Zoroastrians are not seen as dhimmi. Furthermore, little distinction is drawn between the types of kuffār (Jews, Christians, and pagans), because "the meaning of jihād is to strive to liberate Muslim lands from the grip of kuffār who usurped them and imposed on them their own laws instead of the law of Allah. These kuffār may be Jews, Christians, both, or pagans . . . kuffār are all alike: capitalists, Communists, Westerners, Easterners, People of the Book, and pagans are not different from one another."[1]

Islamic law, unlike Western laws of war, does not recognize non-combatants per se as inviolable. While all those whom it is forbidden to harm are non-combatants, not all non-combatants are immune from harm by virtue of that status. The reasoning behind refraining from unnecessarily killing a non-combatant is more in line with the general principle of not causing unnecessary damage and not destroying what may be the spoils of war and hence the property of the Muslims: animals should not be killed unless it is necessary for the war effort, and fruit trees are not to be cut down.

Four main categories of enemies emerge from the legal discussions: combatants during combat, who must be killed; combatants after combat who have been taken prisoner; non-combatants during combat; and non-combatants after combat who have been taken prisoner. These categories focus on levels of inviolability. The first is those who enjoyed immunity (*'iṣma*) and therefore were classified as immune, "whose blood is prohibited" (*ḥarām al-dam*), or "a soul that Allah has forbidden to kill" (*nafs ḥarāma Allah qatlaha*), including Muslims and non-Muslims who have treaties with the Muslims that must be respected: allies (*mu'ahidūn*), travelers with safe passage (*musta'min*), and dhimmi. The second category is those who ought not be killed, including women and children (because they are property of the Muslims), the aged, the mentally retarded, cripples (but only those whose handicap clearly precludes their participation in battle), monks (but only those in cloisters). The third category is those about whom there was discretion whether they would be killed, kept as slaves, or freed (with or without ransom).

An important guideline for treating the enemy, according to clas-

1. Fatwā: Sheikh Yousuf Qaradawi, "Spending Zakah Money on Jihād," 20 March 2003, www.islamonline.net/fatwā/english/FatwāDisplay.asp?hFatwāID = 18235.

sic Islamic jurisprudence, involves the distinction between those individuals who may be able to fight in the future and those who could not pose a threat to Muslims. In fact, this distinction is fraught with ambiguity. Early jurists agreed on the ruling prohibiting the killing of women and children but not regarding the aged or monks (whom the Qur'an specifically prohibited killing). In addition, the various schools of jurisprudence disagreed over the reasons for killing. Whereas most of the Hanifi scholars justified killing only those who may endanger the Muslims (and therefore forbade killing of women, children, and aged people), the Shafi'i scholars, for the most part, justified killing pagans. This ambiguity provides a sound basis for today's radicals who kill civilians, and raise profound difficulties for moderates searching for grounds forbidding such acts.

The most important category of enemies is the class of those who should be killed. There is a consensus that this includes all enemy soldiers during battle. Islamic law prohibits refraining from killing enemy combatants (*ahl al-qitāl*) or taking prisoners during the battle, until the enemy army has been vanquished.[2] The controversy begins over the definitions of "during the battle" and "soldiers," given that the present defensive jihād is viewed as an ongoing battle and that all members of the enemy society are classified as soldiers because they contribute to the enemy's war effort. This rationale is stressed in the case of Israelis and occasionally extended to other Western nationalities.[3]

Contemporary *fatwās* tend to focus on those categories usually defined in modern western society as protected by the laws of war—non-combatant civilians, women, children, the elderly, and clergy.

2. Fatwā: Sheikh Yousuf Al-Qaradawi, "Islam's Stance on Killing Captives," 17 May 2004, www.islamonline.net/fatwā/english/FatwāDisplay.asp?hFatwāID = 114486. *Al-Said Sabiq-fiqh al-Sunnah*, Vol. 3 (Beirut: Shirkat ibna' Sharif al'Ansari, 2002), pp. 63–64. 'Abdalla 'Azzam, *al-jihād-adāb wa ahkām* (On jihād, morals and rules) (n.p.: Matbu'at al-jihād, 1987), pp. 41–53.

3. Ella Landau-Tasseron, "Non-Combatants: Some Muslim Legal Views," unpublished paper.

The legal debate among Islamic scholars does not, however, usually focus on the status of these people as non-combatants per se, but on their inclusion in categories that are idiosyncratic to Islamic law. Thus, scholars are asked such questions as, "Is the bombing of pizza parlors and other civilian targets by Palestinian Muslims considered a legitimate form of jihād? Can you provide relevant citations from the Qur'an or ḥadīth that argue one side or the other?"[4] Are non-Muslim residents of Muslim countries considered dhimmi? And are tourists who enter Muslim countries carrying visas musta'min or citizens of non-Muslim countries that have signed international agreements with Muslim countries considered mu'ahadin and therefore protected?

Fatwās issued by establishment 'ulamā usually insist on total protection of these categories. Hence, the Mufti of Egypt, Dr. 'Ali Guma', emphasized in his rulings that foreigners, and certainly Europeans who support the Muslims, should be protected when traveling through or residing in Muslim lands because their visas accord them immunity as musta'min.[5] This, however, does not extend to kuffār whose home countries have been classified as dār al-ḥarb.

Traditionally, those who may be spared include monks and clergy (albeit only when they are clearly not a danger to the Muslims—for example, recluses). Such exceptions, however, have been discarded in the course of the jihāds of Algeria and the Philippines, where priests, monks, and nuns are popular targets. Few fatwās directly address this issue.

Many jihād fatwās justify killing certain protected persons by portraying them as excluded from the general category of protection and thus unqualified for lenient treatment. Such justifications take two forms. First, the traits of such persons are cited in the Qur'an and

4. Fatwā to Sheikh Faysal Mawlawi, "Attacking Civilians in Martyr Operations," 26October2003,www.islamonline.net/fatwā/english/FatwāDisplay.asp?hFatwāID=4 6143.

5. Fatwā: Dr. 'Ali Guma', *MEMRI, Special Dispatch Series* 580, http://memri .org/bin/articles.cgi?Page=archives&Area=sd&ID=SP58003.

ḥadīth or are seen as similar to groups that were accorded harsh treatment by the Prophet and his Companions. The best-known of these descriptions equate Jews (and occasionally Christians) with apes and pigs—lowly and impure animals in Islam. Second, such persons are identified as polytheists or atheists, with democracy sometimes defined as a polytheistic religion associating other deities with God, thus denying God's uniqueness and allowing humans to overrule God's law. Under such a definition, "democratists"[6]—like the polytheists of seventh-century Arabia—must either accept Islam or be put to the sword. Equating democracy with polytheism echoes the ideas of Sayyid Qutb in his manifesto "In the Shadow of the Qur'an," where he defines Jahiliyya as the rule of man over man instead of the rule of God.[7]

The targeting of civilians is justified in a number of fatwās on the basis of a number of arguments. First, while it is true that killing women, children, and the aged is prohibited, this prohibition derived in the days of the Prophet from their inability to fight the Muslims. In modern warfare, physical stamina is less necessary and therefore these groups may sometimes be considered legitimate targets, including women who take part in the fighting, witness the fighting, give council to the fighters, or deal in propaganda.[8] The ḥadīth that is widely quoted as authority for the prohibition on killing women (the Prophet saw a woman dead and said, "She should not have been killed; she could not have fought") is interpreted as meaning that, had she been able to fight, she should have been killed.

Targeting of monks and clergy is also a matter for debate in fatwās

6. Sivan, *Radical Islam*, p. 22

7. See writings and fatwās by Asem al-Burqawi (Abu Muhammad al-Maqdisi), a Salafi Palestinian, leader of the Bay'at al-Imām group, who became one of bin Laden's open spokesmen. The fatwās were published on his website www.maqdese.com, which has been taken off the Internet. For a discussion of the subject, see Jonathan D. Halevi, "Al-Qaeda's Intellectual Legacy, New Radical Islamic Thinking Justifying the Genocide of Infidels," *Jerusalem Viewpoints* 508 (2003).

8. Discussion about 'ulamā', *Al-Watan* (Kuwait), 31 August 2002.

on jihād due to the above-mentioned stipulation regarding this category. Mujahidin groups in Mindanao in the Philippines and in Algeria have habitually brutally murdered monks, nuns, and other Christian clergy. Al-Qa'ida has also targeted religious figures and symbols in its plans to assassinate Pope John Paul II in Manila (1994), to attack synagogues in North Africa, and to attack churches and other Christian religious sites on New Year's Eve, 2003. Such attacks on religious targets, including those in the Israeli-Palestinian conflict, seem inconsistent with explicit rulings in the Qur'an and ḥadīth. Few 'ulamā have ruled on the subject, leaving it to the gray area of practice. However, a Belgian convert to Islam, Jean Michot (Nasserdin Lebatelier), revived a fatwā from ibn Taymiya that permits killing clergy.[9] The leitmotif of the conflict between Islam and the Crusaders strengthens the legitimacy of killing clergy. If the war is between Islam and the forces of Christendom attempting to eradicate Islam from the hearts of Muslims, then the "soldiers" of Christendom are, first and foremost, the clergy.

Another argument is that the participationn of citizens in democratic processes justifies targeting them. It is claimed that since in Israeli society women have the right to vote they are combatants because they help provide the leaders who are waging war against the Muslims.[10] The U.S. citizen is also considered a combatant because of his "connection to his government, or because he supports it with money or opinion or counsel as is customary in their political regime."[11] The 9/11 attacks were justified because "every decision taken by the kāfir state, America, particularly those that relate to war, is based on public opinion through referendum and/or voting in the House of Representatives or the Senate. Every American, having par-

9. Bonney, *Jihād*, p. 122.

10. Discussion about the legitimacy of killing women, *Al-Watan* (Kuwait), 31 August 2001.

11. Sheikh Ali bin Khdheir al-Khdeir, *MEMRI, Special Dispatch* 333, 18 January 2002. See also Abu Muhammad al-Maqdesi, *"Al-dimikratiya-Dīn"* (Democracy is a religion), undated.

ticipated in this opinion poll and having voted regarding the war, is considered a combatant or at least a party to the war."[12]

A fourth argument that justifies killing civilians is that in modern warfare it is impossible to make a clear distinction between combatants and noncombatants because war is total and the entire populace is involved. Any attempt to make that distinction (and thus refrain from killing women and children) may make it impossible to fight at all, resulting in the "paralysis of jihād."[13] Although in principle one should not kill children and the elderly, if they are killed, it is the result of military necessity.[14]

The distinction between combatants and civilians is, in any case, irrelevant in the case of Israel, since its society is regarded as "militaristic in nature" because both men and women serve in the army and can be drafted at any moment, and their children will grow up to fight the Muslims. According to one fatwā, the civilian who occupies land in a state of war or works in such a country is a combatant; everyone in Israel, therefore, is fair game. One is also permitted to kill an Israeli traveling abroad because he is a combatant and "spreads corruption [fasād] throughout the face of the earth." Even a diplomat's blood is permitted—which does not mean he must be killed, only that his killing is permitted.[15] An earlier fatwā issued by twenty-eight scholars from al-Azhar decreed that killing large numbers of Israeli civilians in Palestinian suicide bombings was the "noblest act of jihād" because Israel is a racist, military state that took Muslim land illegally by force. Hence, there is no need to distinguish between soldiers and civilians.[16] This is also true for all Westerners

12. Fatwā: Sheikh Hammoud Al-Uqlaa Ash-Shuaybi, "Fatwā on Events Following 11 September 2001," 17 September 2001, www.jihādonline.bravepages.com/o qla.htm.

13. Fatwā: Sheikh Hammoud bin al-'Okla al-Shuweibi, 17 September 2001.

14. Sheikh Yousuf Qaradawi to Al-Ahram (Egypt), 3 February 2001.

15. Fatwā: Dr. 'Ali Guma', MEMRI, Special Dispatch Series 580 (2003), http://memri.org/bin/articles.cgi?Page=archives&Area=sd&ID=SP58003.

16. Jonathan D. Halevi, "Al-Qaeda's Intellectual Legacy, New Radical Islamic Thinking Justifying the Genocide of Infidels," Jerusalem Viewpoints 508, 1 December 2003.

working in U.S.-occupied Iraq and Afghanistan, including all those clearly affiliated with the enemy state—in the military forces, embassies, military airports, and so on.

The justifications radical Sheikhs give for the attacks of 9/11 draw on almost all of the above arguments. For example, in November 2001, Saudi sheikh 'Abd al-'Aziz bin Salih al-Jarbou' published a fatwā on the Islamic legal perception of the September 11 events,[17] according to which the sin of the West is in its encouraging the apostasy of the Muslims. He goes on to justify the attacks on the grounds that the West supports so-called moderate Islam, which "accepts the submission to America and to the West and is glad to live in accordance with their way of life [that] grants America the legitimacy to spread its hegemony over the entire world . . . approves the service of the American Muslim in the military forces, in order to fight other Muslims . . . and does not prohibit what Allah and the Prophet forbade."

Another opinion supporting the attacks was that of Saudi sheikh Safar 'Abd Al-Rahman Al-Hawali, who justified them as a legitimate retaliation for the American attack on al-Qa'ida bases following the bombing of the American embassies in Nairobi and Dar a-Salaam. Furthermore, according to Sheikh Al-Hawali, the targets of the 9/11 attacks were neither innocent nor civilian: the Pentagon, he said, (quoting Gore Vidal!) is "Hell and a nest of Satans," a den of spies, and a Mafia nest, whereas the World Trade Center was a "center of usury and money laundering."[18]

A third Saudi radical, Sheikh Ali bin Khdheir Al-Khdheir, focused on the "specious" illegality of targeting civilians. According to bin Khdheir, "those victims were . . . unbelieving Americans who must not be sorrowed over because the kāfir American is considered a combatant due to his connection to his government or because he

---

17. Abd al-'Aziz bin Salih al-Jarbou', *"Al-Ta'sīl limashru'iyyāt ma jara li-amrīkā min tadmār"* (The legal perception of the destruction that happened to America), 10 November 2001, www.almaqdese.com.23/8/1422H.

18. Quoted in Al-Afif Al-Akhahdar, "Is There a Response to a Fatwā Inciting to Crime?" *Al-Hayat* (London), 13 January, 2002.

supports it with money or opinion or counsel, as is customary in their political regime. . . . It is permissible to kill the combatants among them, as well as those who are noncombatants, for example, the aged man, the blind man, and the dhimmi."[19]

After 9/11, similar arguments also appeared in the detailed justification issued by al-Qa'ida for the attacks on the United States, which the organization published (April 24, 2002). This document determines that the United States has never been "dār al-'ahd" (a country with which the Muslims have a treaty), but rather "dār al-ḥarb," and should therefore be considered at war with the Muslims and thus responsible for attacks on Muslims around the world—from Palestine to Iraq, Bosnia-Herzegovina, Kashmir, Chechnya, and East Timor.[20] The argument permitting the killing of Israelis is then extended to Americans. Scholars who define Israeli civilians as *ahl al-qitāl* (combatants who must be killed)and permit "martyrdom operations" against them in Palestine must allow the same in America or risk being inconsistent, for "how can one permit the killing of the branch and not permit the killing of the supporting trunk?"

The al-Qa'ida document also rejects the argument that the attacks were illegal because "Allah forbids killing" women, children, and the elderly, as the "prohibition of the blood of women, children, and elders is not absolute." It lists seven circumstances—only one of which need apply—in which it is permitted to kill such individuals: (1) for reciprocity, when Muslim civilians have been killed by that enemy; (2) when they are mixed together with combatants and it is not possible to differentiate between them; (3) if they have assisted in combat, whether in deed, word, or mind; (4) when it is necessary in order to burn the enemy's strongholds or fields so as to weaken

19. "The Role of Fatwās in Incitement to Terrorism" *MEMRI, Special Dispatch Series* 333 (2002).

20. "*Bayān min Qa'idat a-Jihād Hawl wasaia al-abtāl wa-mashrou'iyāt 'āmaliyāt New York wa-Washinton*" (A statement from Qaidat al-jihād regarding the mandates of the heroes and the legality of the operations in New York and Washington), 24 April 2002, www.almeshkat.net/vb/showthread.php?threadid=1816; also at www .mepc.org/public_asp/journal_vol10/alqaeda.html.

its strength; (5) when using heavy weapons that do not distinguish between combatants and protected ones; (6) when the enemy is shielded by women or children; and (7) to "teach a lesson" to an enemy that has violated a treaty with the Muslims (based on the behavior of the Prophet with Bani Qariza).

Other al-Qa'ida-affiliated writings call the attacks on New York and Washington "raids" (*ghazwah*), alluding to the pre-Islamic Arab tribe's forays that were incorporated into the Islamic doctrine of jihād.[21] The justification for such "raids" is not that they are part of a campaign to occupy territory but rather that they are part of an effort to strike fear into the hearts of the enemy. These documents deviate from the attitude of "regular Muslims," who claim that "we are not against jihād, but jihād has its rules"[22] and that the raids must follow those rules. The main argument the documents attempt to refute is that the attacks caused the death of innocents and "inviolable" souls (including Muslims, women, and children) and were therefore prohibited. The counterargument—based on a list of circumstances under which it is permitted to kill inviolable persons—includes when the killing is "responding in kind" (retaliation) to the killing of Muslims by the enemy; when such persons support a war against Muslims morally or financially; when Muslims "raid" the enemy, making it impossible to distinguish between combatants and "inviolable" persons; and when breaking through the defenses of the enemy makes it impossible to make a distinction.[23]

Targeting Muslims

The al-Qa'ida documents mentioned above also discuss whether attacks that also kill Muslims are illegal, for under Islamic law if two

21. See the collection of articles and studies in *Ghazwat 11 Sibtimbir* (The raid of 11 September), *Kitab al-Ansar li-mowajahat al-ḥarb al-salabiyya* 1 (Books of al-Ansur confronting the Crusader War 1) (September 2002).

22. Al-Ansari, Said a-Din, "Ghazwat New York wa-Washinton" (The Raids of New York and Washington), in *Ghazwat 11 Siptimbir*, p. 9.

23. Ibid., pp. 11–12.

Muslims struggle in battle and one kills the other, both are condemned to hell because each intended to kill another Muslim. As in the case of suicide attacks, however, it is the intent that determines the legitimacy of the act. Because only kuffār should be within the target area, Muslims were not killed intentionally but were collateral casualties. Thus, refraining from attacks for fear of killing Muslims would have resulted in a "suspension of jihād," which is a sin. Furthermore, Muslims who are present at such a target may be assisting the enemy; if they are guilty of such a crime, they have earned their punishment. Finally, the document states that, if the attacks were condemned, then the harm to the large group of Muslims would be greater than that incurred by the death of a few.

The wars in Afghanistan and Iraq have called attention to the issue of the collateral killing of Muslims in the course of a jihād operation. The debate focuses on the concept of *tirs* or *tattarus* (literally, "shielding"), which originated in the twelfth-century essay "Al-Mustasfa" (The Place of Purification) by Abu-Hamed al-Ghazali, in which he endorses "using ordinary Muslims as human shields for Islamic combatants against infidel fighters" (later elaborated by Sheikh ibn Taymiyya in order to deal with the rules for fighting the Mongols). Tattarus was revived by the al-Qa'ida ideologue Ayman al-Zawahayri in his essay "The Rule for Suicide-Martyr Operations," in which he justifies killing Muslims in the course of jihād.[24] A number of modern scholars[25] have expanded on this, arguing that the broader interest of the ummah requires expelling the U.S.-led forces from

24. Ayman al-Zawahiri, *Arkān al-'āmaliyyat al-istishhādiya.*

25. These include the Egyptian Sheikh Yusuf al-Qaradawi and the Saudi Sheikh Hammoud al-Uqla al-Shu'weibi, Sheikh Ali al-Khudhair, Sheikh Nasser al-Fahd, Sheikh Amad al-Khalidi, Sheikh Abu-Muhammad al-Maqdasi, Sheikh Abu-Basir al-Tartussi, and Sheikh Safar al-Hawali. See their fatwās in Fatwā by Shu'eibi, www .palestine-info/arabic/fatawa/alfatawa/hmadbnshaabe.htm; and Fatwā by Suleiman bin Nasser al-'Alwan, http://66.34.76.88/SuliemaAlwan/AmalieatFidaieh.htm. Also see Sheikh Othman Muhammad Gharib al-Hashemi (Iraq), who presents the case that tattarus is permitted only if there is no other way to kill kuffār who must be killed, http://198.65.147.194/Arabic/news/2004–06/29/article10.shtml.

Iraq and that the killing of innocent Iraqis should be of no concern to the combatants, whose place in Paradise in assured.[26]

A more sophisticated justification is on a tape by the al-Qa'ida leader in Iraq, Abu Mus'ab al-Zarqawi:

> The servants of Allah who perform jihād to elevate the word (laws) of Allah are permitted to use any and all means necessary to strike the active unbeliever combatants for the purpose of killing them, snatch their souls from their body, cleanse the earth from their abomination, and lift their trial and persecution of the servants of Allah. The goal must be pursued even if the means to accomplish it affect both the intended active fighters and unintended passive ones such as women, children, and any other passive category specified by our jurisprudence. . . . This permissibility extends to situations in which Muslims may get killed if they happen to be with or near the intended enemy and if it is not possible to avoid hitting them or separate them from the intended Kafirs. Although spilling sacred Muslim blood is a grave offense, it is not only permissible but it is mandated in order to prevent more serious adversity from happening, stalling, or abandoning jihād . . . handing over the land and people to the unbelievers . . . Muslims will be forced to live by Kafir rules [and] . . . Islam will be altered, modified, and replaced with another form that will be totally different from that which was revealed to the one who was sent with the sword.

The issue of tattarus raises additional legal questions. For example, does a mujāhid have to obtain a legal dispensation for every act of jihād that entails tattarus? Most scholars identified with the jihād movement see no need for such a complication, leaving the specific case to the discretion of the individual mujāhid. A number of scholars, however, are disturbed by the implications of a blanket tattarus. Thus, even the radical Shiite Sheikh Hussein Fadlallah, the spiritual

26. Amir Taheri, "To Kill or Not To Kill," *New York Post*, 10 June 2005; and Robert Spencer, "Abu Zarqawi, Holy Man," 31 May 2005, www.frontpagemag.com/Articles/ReadArticle.asp?ID = 18242.

leader of Hezbollah, warns that such cases must be referred to a higher scholar. Others go further, limiting tattarus to situations of collateral killing in a conflict between regular armies or killing Muslims who are in the hands of the enemy or denying the validity of tattarus altogether.[27]

Suicide Attacks

The arsenal of permitted and forbidden weapons allowed by traditional Islamic laws of jihād was limited to those that existed in the seventh century. The only clear prohibition is in a ḥadīth that relates to punishment by fire, which, the Prophet forbade: "no one punishes with fire, save the Lord of the fire (Allah)."[28] No Islamic scholar, however, has deduced from that prohibition that modern explosives that kill "by fire" are prohibited by Islam, although it has been discussed in a few fatwās, including questions regarding the terrorist attacks of 9/11, in which many of the victims burned to death.

The weapon most widely identified with Islamic terrorism is the suicide bomber. Much of the Western discussion of this relates to the intentional targeting of innocent civilians and the Muslim subculture of adulation of the martyr. In Islamic legal discourse, however, the main question is its apparent contradiction of the Islamic prohibition against a Muslim's taking his own life. The Qur'an does not take a clear stand on suicide, but the verses "He alone grants life and death" (10:56) and "Do not cast yourselves into destruction with your own hands" (2:195) are frequently interpreted as prohibiting suicides. In addition to a number of ḥadīths in which the Prophet

27. These include the Shiite Ayatollah Ozma Ali Sistani of Najaf, Sheikh al-Azhar Muhammad Tantawi of Cairo, and Jassem al-Shumri and Abd al-Muhsin al-Ubaikan from Saudi Arabia. See "Fatwā by a Group of Muftis," 23 May 2005, www.islamonline.net/fatwāapplication/arabic/display.asp?hFatwāID = 124782 and www.alshirazi.com/rflo/m_motijadedah/part8/b/3.htm.

28. *Sunnan Abu Daoud*, Book 14, Number 2667.

condemns suicides to hell, Islam has traditionally strictly prohibited suicide, equating it with denying the unity (*tawḥīd*) of Allah or rebelling against his will (in contradiction to the essence of Islam, which is submission to the will of God).[29] Consequently, a major issue for many contemporary fatwās relating to jihād is whether these attacks are martyrdom, and hence a legitimate tactic for jihād, or suicide, and therefore forbidden.

Scholars who categorically forbid suicide attacks are few, however. Even fewer rule that such attacks are suicide in the Islamic sense and thus sentence their perpetrators to fire in the afterlife or that suicide attacks come under the category of "killing one's self" and are therefore illegal and "have nothing to do with jihād on the 'path of Allah.'"[30] Some reject the claim that such attacks are justified by the benefit they bring to Muslims, saying that they do not benefit Islam because even if the bomber kills tens or hundreds or thousands of kuffār, the enemy will retaliate and kill many more Muslims.[31]

But those who justify martyrdom operations find support in the Qur'an and ḥadīth, which are replete with praise for the mujāhid who endangers himself knowing that he is going to be killed. This attitude is epitomized in the Qur'an 9:38: "O you who believe! What is the matter with you, that, when you are asked to go forth in the cause of Allah, you cling heavily to the earth? Do you prefer the life

29. Franz Rosenthal, "On Suicide in Islam," *Journal of the American Oriental Society* 66 (1946): 253.

30. The Saudi Grand Mufti, Sheikh 'Abd al-'Aziz bin 'Abdallah All al-Sheikh, "*Al-Sharq al-Awsat*," 21 April 2001. This statement was not a formal fatwā and was not formally endorsed as such; it seems to have been a reaction to American pressure in the wake of the bombing of the U.S.S. *Cole* on October 12, 2000. An exceptional position is that of Sheikh Muhammad Hisham Kabbami, chairman of the Islamic Supreme Council of America, who debates the legal arguments that support justifiers of suicide attacks. Muhammad Hisham Kabbani, "Principles of Leadership in War and Peace," lecture at the World International Conference of Islamic Scholars, Jakarta, December 21, 2004, pp. 38–43.

31. Sheikh ibn 'Utheymeen, *Riyaadhus-Saaliheen* 1:165–166, translated on www.fatwā-online.com/fataawa/worship/jihaad/jih004/0010915_1.htm. Sheikh 'Utheymneen,though, had justified Hamas suicide operations in the mid 1990s.

of this world to the Hereafter? But little is the comfort of this life, as compared with the Hereafter." It is also heard in the verse "Certainly you desired death before you met it" (3:143).[32]

Nevertheless, the active adulation of death is not a central element of mainstream Islam, although modern fatwās frequently use historical precedents to justify martyrdom operations. The favorable attitude toward intentional martyrdom "in Allah's cause" was a hallmark of the Khawarij sect. As noted above, however, this sect was denounced by its mainstream contemporaries, and its name became a pejorative for unacceptable religious extremism. Even the Shi'ah—with its elaborate martyrology of the Imāms 'Ali, Hussein, and Hassan—shied away from seeing those events as legitimizing the seeking of death.

Furthermore, the historical Islamic martyr did not kill himself but rather placed himself in a situation in which he would most likely be killed and thereby did not violate the Qur'anic prohibition on suicide. The targets of the suicide terrorist of ancient times were also different: officials of the ruling class and armed (Muslim) enemies. The true predecessor of modern suicide terrorism is most likely the Shiite-Nizari sect of the Assassins, which existed in the twelfth and thirteenth centuries. The members of the sect, who sacrificed themselves to kill enemy leaders, were called *fidayun* ("self-sacrificers")—a term later used by the secular Palestinian organizations for their militants. Even these fidayun, however, did not kill themselves. They put themselves in a position in which they were killed by the enemy after having accomplished their mission.[33] In modern Islam, the founder of the Muslim Brotherhood, Sheikh Hassan al-Banna, took this a step further, introducing "the art of death (*fan al-mawt*)."[34] This concept was developed further in "an oath of alle-

32. These verses are widely quoted by radical Islamic organizations and repeated again and again in al-Qa'ida recruitment videotapes.

33. Farhad Daftary, *The Assassin Legends: Myths of the Isma'ilis* (New York: Tauris, 1995), pp. 34–35.

34. Mitchell, *The Society of the Muslim Brotherhood*, p. 207. Al-Bana also coined the concept "industry of death" (*san'at al-mawt*) as a positive concept: "Death is

giance with death" (*bay'ah*, relating to a person's oath to his leader), prevalent in the writings emerging from the Afghani mujāhidin. This ideology presents death as a "betrothal with martyrdom," (*'ars al-shahada*) not a necessary evil in war. The willingness, even the desire, to die in Allah's cause is the only way to achieve victory.

Modern 'ulamā began addressing the legitimacy of martyrdom operations in the wake of their use by the Lebanese Hezbollah and the Palestinian Islamic jihād. In the absence of leading scholars inside Palestine (though Hamas published legal treatises justifying suicide bombing), scholars from Egypt and the gulf supported the phenomenon. The legal foundation for martyrdom attacks in the Israeli context had already been established at the time of the 9/11 attacks. Some attempts to distinguish between attacks against Israeli civilians (permitted and even recommended), and attacks against Americans and other Westerners (prohibited) seem specious. They are based on the definition of Israel as an enemy toward whom jihād is an individual duty, as opposed to the United States, which, although hostile to Muslims, cannot be defined as yet as an enemy.[35] This argument, of course, falls apart the moment it is claimed that the United States, like Israel, is occupying Muslim lands and even attempting to introduce its own mores into those lands (in the form of democracy in the "Broader Middle East," for example).

Numerous other arguments have been advanced to justify suicide attacks. These include the verse in the Qur'an (2:195): "And spend yourselves in the way of Allah, and do not cast yourselves into destruction with your own hands." This is traditionally interpreted as

an industry like any other industry. There are those people who know how to die with honor and to choose an honorable place and time [to die]. He sells his blood for the highest price and earns in return the highest profit." Hassan al-Bana, "*Sana'at al-Mawt*" (The industry of death) quoted in *Al-Imām al-Shahid yataḥadīth ila Shabab al-'aālim al-Islami* (The martyr imam speaks to the youth of the Islamic world) (Beirut: Dar al-Qalam, 1974), pp. 129–132.

35. Fatwā: Sheikh Mawlawi "Does the U.S. Biased Policy Against Palestinians Make Her Dar Harb?" 8 October 2002, www.islamonline.net/fatwā/english/FatwāDisplay.asp?hFatwāID = 52392.

prohibiting suicide but it is actually a tautology: *not* spending oneself "in the way of Allah" is tantamount to "casting one's self into destruction."[36] One fatwā, which interprets that phrase as "investing money and giving up jihād," is based on a ḥadīth in which the verse emerged in response to the loss of heart of the Ansār (the non-Muslim "supporters," who had joined the Muslims) who preferred to forsake the jihād and go home to invest their money, thus "casting themselves into destruction."[37]

Other prevalent arguments invoked in support of suicide attacks involve precedents set by the Companions of the Prophet who charged into the ranks of the kuffār knowing they would be killed;[38] the centrality of "intention" (*niya*) in determining if the right or wrong of a certain deed transforms the act of suicide into an act of martyrdom;[39] and the absence of alternative tactics. Thus, although Muslims do not have the military power of their adversaries, their martyrdom attacks may be seen as "cost-effective."[40]

A number of fatwās quote early mujtāhidūn who ruled that a Muslim may give up his life intentionally in jihād if his act hurts the enemy, dispirits him, or encourages Muslims. But if he is not sure that such an act will kill the enemy, he is "discouraged from perform-

36. Fatwā: Sheikh Faysal Mawlawi, 28 April 2001.

37. Fatwā: "Abu Ruqaiyah," *Nida ul-Islam*, December—January 1996–1997.

38. Some examples frequently used as analogies are the cases of Ja'far ibn Abu Taleb and Zayd bin al-Haritha.

39. Fatwā: Sheikh Suleiman bin Nasser al-'Alwan, "Hukm al-'Amaliyat al-Istsh-hadiya," 14.6.1423 Hijri (24 August 2002). Based on a ḥadīth that states, "Actions are but by intentions."

40. Fatwā: Islamic Fiqh Council, "Martyr Operations or Suicide," 24 January 2004, www.islamonline.net/fatwa/english/FatwaDisplay.asp?hFatwaID=91481. The council is affiliated with the OIC. The fatwās were issued during its fourteenth session, held in Duha (Qatar), 11–16 January 2003: "Martyr operations are a form of jihād, and carrying out those operations is a legitimate right that has nothing to do with terrorism or suicide. Those operations become obligatory when they become the only way to stop the aggression of the enemy, defeat it, and grievously damage its power."

ing it."[41] Senior Islamic scholars justify Palestinian suicide as a necessary tactic in light of the strategic weakness of the Muslims in their conflict with their enemy. Thus, some 'ulamā began describing suicide bombing not only as "belonging to jihād" but as "the best jihād for the sake of Allah."[42]

Such positions have been tempered by political considerations. Consider, for example, the changes in the rulings of Sheikh al-Azhar, Mohammad Sayed Tantawi. In 2001, Tantawi issued a fatwā stating that martyrdom operations are "self-defense and a kind of martyrdom, as long as the intention behind them is to kill the enemy's soldiers and not women or children."[43] A year later he issued a ruling saying that "every martyrdom operation against any Israeli, *including children, women, and teenagers*, is a legitimate act according to [Islamic] religious law, and an Islamic commandment, until the people of Palestine regain their land and cause the cruel Israeli aggression to retreat [emphasis added]."[44]

Scholars who categorically forbid suicide attacks are few. A few rule that such attacks are suicide in the Islamic sense and thus sentence their perpetrators to fire in the afterlife, arguing that suicide attacks come under the category of "killing one's self and are therefore illegal and have nothing to do with jihād on the 'path of Allah.' "[45] Some also reject the claim that they are justified by a utilitarian cal-

41. *Nida ul-Islam*, December–January 1996–1997.

42. Fatwā: Sheikh 'Ali bin Khdheir al-Khdheir, "*Hukm al-'Amaliyyat al-istishhād-iyya*" (The law of martyrdom operations), 14 5.1423 Hijri (24 July 2004).

43. Yotam Feldner, "Debating the Religious, Political and Moral Legitimacy of Suicide Bombings, Part 1: The Debate Over Religious Legitimacy," *MEMRI, Inquiry and Analysis Series* 53 (2001).

44. *MEMRI, Inquiry and Analysis Series* 363 (2002).

45. The Saudi Grand Mufti, Sheikh 'Abd al-'Aziz bin 'Abdallah All al-Sheikh, "*Al-Sharq al-Awsat*," 21 April, 2001. This statement was not a formal fatwā and was not formally endorsed as such; it seems to have been a reaction to American pressure in the wake of the bombing of the U.S.S. *Cole* on October 12, 2000. An exceptional position is that of Sheikh Muhammad Hisham Kabbami, chairman of the Islamic Supreme Council of America, who debates the legal arguments that support justifiers of suicide attacks. Muhammad Hisham Kabbani, "Principles of Leadership

culus. This is not because it is not a valid argument, but because in fact these specific acts do not pass the test of cost effectiveness. In the final analysis, they do not benefit Islam, since even if the bomber kills tens or hundreds of thousands of kuffar, the enemy will retaliate and kill many more Muslims.

The analogy to examples from the history of Islam is also challenged. It is claimed that while it is true that in the past, Islamic law authorized army commanders to permit Muslim warriors to storm the enemy, knowing the warriors had no chance of surviving, it was not permitted for the individual to decide for himself. Such a decision could only be taken by the ruler or the caliph, who could weigh the benefits and damages of such an act. Otherwise the suicide attack could condemn its practitioner either to an eternity in the fire, or to be among those residing in the fire until they are freed from hell on the Day of Judgment.[46]

Nevertheless, even those sheikhs who prohibit suicide bombing admit that the reward or punishment of the perpetrator in the next life will be according to his real intention, which is something only God knows. Thus, Sheikh Muhammad ibn Saleh 'Uthaymeen rules that "what some people do regarding activities of suicide, tying explosives to themselves and then approaching disbelievers and detonating them amongst them, then this is a case of suicide—and Allah's refuge is sought. So whoever commits suicide, then he will be considered eternally to hell-fire, remaining there forever." The sheikh goes on to say that though the suicide bomber will not receive the rewards of a martyr, he may be saved from hellfire "if [he] has done this based upon misinterpretation, thinking that it is permissible, then we hope that he will be saved from sin, but as for martyrdom being written for him, then no, since he has not taken the path

in War and Peace," lecture at the World International Conference of Islamic Scholars, Jakarta, December 21, 2004, pp. 38–43.

46. Fatwā: Imām Muhammad Naasir-ud Deen Al-Albaanee, "Suicide Bombings in the Scales of Islamic Law," in Abu Saalih, Muhammad Zorkane Al-Maghribee, *Al-Masjid al-Aqsa: The Path to Its Freedom* (New York: SSNA, 2005).

of martyrdom. But whoever performs ijtihad and errs will receive a single reward."[47]

The claim that martyrdom purges the martyr of all his sins is based on numerous traditions, according to which the martyr is admitted into Paradise by virtue of his martyrdom in jihād. The martyr is absolved of all his sins, even adultery and theft, from the first gush of his blood, and is transported directly to Paradise without having to be interrogated within his body by the angels. (Such beliefs may explain the seemingly un-Islamic behavior, including drinking alcohol, of the September 11 terrorists on the eve of their mission.) This tradition has also demolished the idea that suicide terrorists could be deterred were they told that their bodies would be defiled by being wrapped in pig skins to prevent their souls from reaching Paradise.

Prisoners and Hostages

Another dilemma that emerges from modern terrorist tactics regards the taking of prisoners (or hostages) and their subsequent execution (a common tactic of terrorist groups and certainly not specific to radical Islamic groups). Such tactics raise a number of legal difficulties, and have resulted in a number of fatwās analyzing the issue. The guidelines they set down are similar:[48] During war, Muslims should not capture enemy soldiers; only after vanquishing the enemy can prisoners be taken.[49] According to the Qur'an, after the enemy has

47. Sheikh ibn 'Utheymeen, *Riyaadhus-Saaliheen*, 1, 165–166. Translated on www.fatwā-online.com/fataawa/worship/jihaad/jih004/0010915_1.htm.

48. Fatwā: Sheikh Yousuf al-Qaradawi, "Enslavement of POWs," 26 May 2004, www.islamonline.net/fatwā/english/FatwāDisplay.asp?hFatwāID=114759; and Fatwā by a group of Muftis, "Islam's Stance on Prisoners of War," 1 June 2003, www.islam online.net/fatwā/english/FatwāDisplay.asp?hFatwāID=55158.

49. According to the Qur'an (8:67), "It is not fitting for a Prophet that he should have prisoners of war until he has thoroughly subdued the land." And (47:4), "So when you meet in battle the kuffār, then smite the necks until when you have overcome them, then make [them] prisoners, and afterwards either set them free as a favor or let them ransom [themselves] until the war terminates."

been captured, there are only two possibilities: either grace or ransom, which may be paid by the families or through indentured work by the prisoners themselves. The ḥadīth offers two more possibilities: enslavement and killing. Some scholars claim that the offer of "grace or ransom" has been abrogated by a later verse (9:5) obliging Muslims to "slay the idolaters wherever you find them."

Abdallah Azzam elaborated on the rules regarding prisoners (after the battle) in his fatwās concerning the morals and rules of jihād. His discussion is of special interest because it focused on the situation in Afghanistan in the 1980s and was, thus, not a theoretical exercise calling on the rulings of earlier generations. Azzam preserves the traditional distinction between women and children, whom "it is not permitted to kill," and men, who are at the mercy of the Imām (in Afghanistan, the leader of the organization or party), who decides whether to free them or to allow them to ransom themselves. Azzam permits, however, killing "Communist prisoners" (because the war was against Communists, this is a wide dispensation) and kuffār who are wounded. The Communist woman must be killed because she is an apostate.[50]

The nature of the U.S.-led campaigns in Iraq and Afghanistan also marked as legitimate targets civilian (including Muslim) personnel who support the "occupation forces." Because of criticism emanating from the Muslim world of the killing of hostages, the Iraqi Islamic group the Secret Islamic Army—the Battalions of the Black Banners requested a fatwā from the Iraqi Sunni Association of Muslim Scholars to decide whether Islam permits kidnapping and killing foreigners who work with the occupation forces, declaring in advance that it would abide by such a fatwā. The association, however, could not reach a decision; its spokesman, Sheikh 'Abd el-Satar 'Abd el-Jabar, announced that such a request calls for profound study and is not an easy task. In the end, no fatwā was issued.[51]

50. Abdallah 'Azzam, *Fi al- jihād Adab wa-Ahkam* (On jihad: morals and rules) (n.p.: Matbuat al- jihād,1987), pp. 41–53.

51. *Al-Watan* (Saudi Arabia), 6 September 2004; and *The Guardian* (UK), 5 September 2004.

The principles of *lex talionis* and reciprocity (*mu'āmila bil-mithl*, "repayment in kind") are central to Islamic law. The principle of "an eye for an eye, a tooth for a tooth, and a soul for a soul" also holds, except that the value of a Muslim is greater than that of a kāfir and, therefore, a Muslim may not be executed for killing a non-Muslim.[52] This principle is also used to rule that the punishment meted out to the kuffār for a wrong committed against the Muslims need not be proportionate, for the life of a Muslim is worth between two and ten times that of a non-Muslim. Thus, according to the radical 'ulamā, per the number of Muslims killed by the infidels under U.S. leadership, Muslims have the right to kill at least four million Americans, half of them children.[53]

Beheading Hostages

Execution by beheading has become a trademark of the radical movements. It was widely implemented by the Abu Sayyaf group in the Philippines in the early 1990s and has been used by the Chechen rebels since the late 1990s. The watershed use of this method by the international jihād groups, however, was the murder of *Wall Street Journal* reporter Daniel Pearl in Pakistan in February 2002. Since then, the beheading of prisoners (mostly civilians) has become increasingly common. The videotaped executions depict religious rituals, with the executioners abiding by regulations stipulated by shari'ah, including identifying the hostages as belligerent kuffār or protected individuals (dhimmi or holders of aman), the permission to kill prisoners (instead of allowing their ransom) during the battle or after it is over, and the form of execution.

The first two questions have already been discussed. The dispensation for killing the hostages is granted because they are accomplices to the kāfir invasion of the Muslim land and therefore are not

52. Friedmann, *Tolerance and Coercion in Islam*, pp. 39–47.

53. Abu Gheith (al-Qa'ida spokesman) at www.alneda.com (the website has been closed down), quoted in *MEMRI, Special Report* 25 (2004): 9.

protected individuals. In the wake of the abduction and murder of journalists, a debate ensued over whether journalists should be protected because their reporting serves the cause of the jihād. Similarly, the abduction of French nationals and nationals of other countries "friendly to the Muslims" was debated as being damaging to general Muslim interests.

The revulsion in the West evoked widespread denials by Islamic scholars that the beheadings are in line with Islamic law. However, decapitation has historically been practiced by radical Islamic groups, including the Sudanese Mahdīsts and rebels against the secular Turkish regime.[54] The groups that engage in the practice today (Abu Mus'ab al-Zarqawi's Al-Tawhid wal-Jihad and others) justify it on the basis of two verses in the Qur'an: (8:12): "I will cast terror in their hearts and strike upon their necks" and (47:4) "When you meet the infidels on the battlefield, strike at their necks until you have crushed them completely and then bind the prisoners." The interpretation is that the act of "striking at their necks" by the mujāhidūn is meant to put fear in the hearts of the enemy and that hostages cannot be considered "prisoners" (who may be ransomed) because the enemy has not been crushed. This echoes the reasoning of the eminent fundamentalist Islamic thinker Abu a'la Mawdudi (a forefather of modern Islamic fundamentalism who was strongly influenced by the Wahhabiya and who strongly influenced the Muslim Brotherhood in the Arab world), who wrote that verse 47:4 is a clear obligation: "By no means should the Muslim take enemy soldiers as captives (until) after the enemy has been completely crushed."[55] That verse is reinforced by the example of the Prophet, who ordered the execution by decapitation of seven hundred men of the Jewish Banu Qurayza tribe in Medina.

---

54. Timothy Furnish, "Beheading in the Name of Islam," *Middle East Quarterly* (Spring 2005): 2.

55. Abu A'la Mawdudi, *The Meaning of the Qur'an*, Vol. 13 (Lahore: Islamic Publications Ltd., 1986), p. 13.

Mutilation of Bodies

A number of fatwās proscribe mutilating enemy bodies, as the Prophet and the first caliphs prohibited the custom of decapitating enemies as proof of their deaths.[56] Here, too, the guiding principles are what the kuffār have been seen to have done to the Muslims.[57] One fatwā on this matter states that Islam prohibits torturing living people and mutilating the dead, even if they are non-Muslims. If, however, the enemies of Islam torture and mutilate Muslims, then the Muslims are permitted to reciprocate. According to the Qur'an (16:126), Allah says: "If you punish, then punish with the like of that by which you were afflicted."[58] An even more general dispensation for mutilating the dead issued from a fatwā by the Saudi Sheikh Omar Abdullah Hassan al-Shihabi, who said that the dead can be mutilated not only as a reciprocal act but also when it serves to "terrorize the enemy" or to "gladden the heart of a Muslim mujāhid."

Mutilating bodies in retaliation for the mutilation of Muslims is derived from the case in which pagans mutilated the body of Hamzah ibn 'Abdul-Muttalib, one of the Prophet's Companions, and the Prophet swore to mutilate seventy pagan corpses in retaliation.[59] The London-based radical Sheikh Hani al-Siba'i justified the mutilation and torture of enemies by the precedent of the Prophet who, as a punishment for stealing sheep, "drove nails and gouged out the eyes of the 'Urayna tribe . . . cut off their opposite arms and legs and

56. Fatwā by Sheikh Yousuf al-Qaradawi, "Mutilating the Dead," 15 May 2004, www.islamonline.net/fatwāapplication/english/display.asp?hFatwāID = 114407.

57. The principle of retribution (qissas) is deeply rooted both in Islamic law and in customary tribal law. In tribal customary law ('urf), the community is held responsible for the acts of its members.

58. Fatwā: Collective fatwā by a group of Muftis, "Mutilating the Dead Bodies in War," 1 April 2004, www.islamonline.net/fatwā/english/FatwāDisplay.asp?hFatwāID = 112837.

59. Fatwā: Sheikh Faysal Mawlawi, Dr. Ahmad Abu-Al-Wafa, Sheikh 'Ikrimah Sabri, 1 April 2004, www.islamonline.net/fatwā/english/FatwāDisplay.asp?hFatwāID = 112837.

threw them into al-Hrara area to die." If the mere crime of thievery warranted such punishment, according to the sheikh, the crimes of the occupiers of Iraq certainly do.[60] Other ḥadīths quoted to justify mutilation are Muhammad's joy upon being served the severed head of his enemy, Abu Hakm, after the battle of Badr against the Meccans, and the mutilation, on his orders, of 'Umaiya bin Khalaf.

Nuclear Weapons

It would seem that the prohibition noted above on punishment by fire should have an even clearer bearing on the use of nuclear weapons. Interestingly, however, this analogy has not been used in any of the wide range of fatwās included in this study. Rather, nuclear weapons have been discussed in the context of the use of weapons of mass destruction in general. The main point of many of the fatwās siding with the legality of nuclear weapons is a Muslim's duty to "defend one's soul," to achieve military superiority over the enemy, to maintain reciprocity—at least—in types of weapons, to deter the enemy, or to "make the enemies of the ummah tremble." Hence, no type of weapon is, by definition, illegal.[61]

The acquisition and use of nuclear weapons has been treated in a number of fatwās for more than a decade, with deliberations distinguishing between obtaining nuclear weapons and actually using them. The prevailing argument, as presented by the Fatwā Committee of al-Azhar, is that as long as nuclear weapons are held by the Muslims' enemies (the United States, Israel, or any other nation) it is the Islamic duty of all Muslim countries to acquire such weapons. A Muslim regime that does not fulfill this duty is a sinner and may

---

60. Hani al-Siba'i to *A.N.B. TV* (22 February 2005), *MEMRI*, http://memritv .org/TRanscript.asp?P1 = 576.

61. Fatwā: Dr. Muzammil Siddiqi, "How Islam Views Possession of Nukes," 15 December 2002, www.islamonline.net/fatwā/english/FatwāDisplay.asp?hFatwāID = 82127.

be guilty of "corruption (fasād) on earth." The aim of having these weapons is, first and foremost, to "make the enemies of the ummah tremble" (*irhab a'ada al-Ummah*—[Qur'an 8:60] the root "r-h-b" used here serves in modern Arabic for the meaning "to terrorize").[62]

The ruling on the use of nuclear weapons, however, derives from different reasoning. Some fatwās take as their point of departure the principle of lex talionis: "In case these nuclear weapons are used against Muslims, it becomes permissible for Muslims to defend themselves using the same weapon, based on the Qur'an (16:126): 'If you punish, then punish with the like of that by which you were afflicted.'"[63] The sheikh of al-Azhar, Muhammad Tantawi, drew an analogy from the ruling of the Caliph Abu Bakr (573–634): "to fight the enemy with a sword if he fights with a sword and . . . with a spear if he fights with a spear." Had Abu Bakr lived today, he would have instructed that, if the enemy uses a nuclear bomb, it is the Muslims' duty to use it as well.[64] Another consideration is that nuclear weapons would kill "souls that Allah has forbidden to kill," such as Muslims, women, children, the elderly, and ascetics in prayer. A twenty-five-page-long fatwā by Saudi sheikh Nasser bin Hamid al-Fahd, issued in May 2003, considers the legal ramifications of using weapons of mass destruction (WMD), even on children and other Muslims, and concludes that using WMD against the United States is obligatory. The behavior of the United States against the Muslims is such that it positively warrants the use of WMD.[65]

62. Fatwā: Sheikh 'alla al-Shanawi by The Al-Azhar Fatwās Committee headed by Sheikh 'Ali Abu al-Hassan, faxed text in handwriting, www.islamonline.net/ Arabic/news/2002–12/23/article06.shtml.

63. Fatwā: Sheikh Faysal Mawlawi, "Using WMD in War: Islamic View," 16 December 2002, www.islamonline.net/fatwā/english/FatwāDisplay.asp?hFatwāID= 52398.

64. www.islamonline.net/iol-arabic/dowalia/alhadath-17–11/alhadath2.asp, 17 November 1999.

65. Sheikh Nasr bin Hamid al-Fahd, "Risālah fi ḥukm istikhdām islihat al-damār al-shāmil did al-kuffār" (A treatise on the legal status of using weapons of mass destruction against infidels) (n.p.:1 May 2003).

In contrast, a number of fatwās outlaw WMD because of their indiscriminate nature, killing "souls that Allah has forbidden to kill" along with the guilty. According to a fatwā by Sheikh Taher Jaber Alwani, the use of WMD is "not permissible" because they do not differentiate between the innocent and the criminal. Sheikh Alwani also objects to their use because Islamic law obliges lex talionis by the kin of a person who is wrongly killed. In the case of WMD, because the innocent will be taken with the guilty, the door opens to an endless cycle of legally justified revenge.[66] Sheikh Qaradawi, adopting a more subtle view, went on record in favor of Muslims acquiring nuclear weapons but ruled that they should be used only as a deterrent, with their actual use forbidden.[67]

The legality of the acquisition of nuclear weapons has been an issue in Shiite Iran as far back as the early 1980s.[68] On his accession to power in 1979, Khomeini ordered the shah's nuclear program suspended, and is said to have issued a fatwā declaring that nuclear weapons are "from Satan." Although we have no specific fatwā by Khomeini rescinding this position, the nuclear program was revived while he was still alive. Nevertheless, his position against nuclear weapons remains in force among many traditional "quietist" clerics, who claim that a consensus among senior clerics prohibiting nuclear weapons (or WMD in general) is "self-evident in Islam," and that is an "eternal law" that cannot be reversed because the basic function of these weapons is to kill innocent people.[69] This ruling was behind the Iranian decision not to use chemical weapons against Iraq during the war.[70] In September 2003, an additional fatwā was issued by the

66. Fatwā: Taher Jaber al-'Alwani, "Using WMD in War: Islamic View," http://islamonline.net/fatwā/english/FatwāDisplay.asp?hFatwāID = 52398.

67. Qaradawi to *Qatari TV*, 18 October 2002.

68. Shmuel Bar, *Iranian Defense Doctrine and Decision Making* (Herzliya: Institute for Policy and Strategy, 2004), p. 51.

69. Ayatollah Montazeri, Interview with *Die Welt*, 9 November 2003.

70. Ayatollah Saanei interviewed by Robert Collier, *San Francisco Chronicle*, 31 October 2003, sec. A, p. 1.

scholars of Qom stating that "nuclear weapons are un-Islamic because they are inhumane."[71] During negotiations between the E-3 nations (the United Kingdom, France, and Germany) and Iran over Iran's nuclear program, the Iranians claimed that the Supreme Leader Ayatollah 'Ali Khamene'i had issued a fatwā prohibiting nuclear weapons. In fact, no such fatwā had been issued.

Jihād and Money

Jihād through the use of one's wealth is deeply entrenched in Islamic tradition,[72] on the basis of the injunction that a Muslim must fight jihād with his soul (*jihād bi-nafs*), with his tongue (*jihād al-lissan or da'wah*), and with his money (*jihād bi-mal*). Therefore, supporting jihād financially is correct and even good for the business of the wealthy supporter. The three main forms of economic jihād discussed in contemporary fatwās are financing the armed jihād and the mujāhidūn; economic boycotts with the aim of weakening the economy of the enemy and strengthening the economy of Muslim countries; and disrupting the economic interests of the enemy by refusing to work with businesses of the enemy, engaging in strikes against them, and so forth.[73]

The call for Muslims to contribute to the jihād of other Muslims is not new. The mufti of Egypt, Hasanayn Muhammad Makhluf, issued a fatwā in April 1948 obliging all Muslims to make financial contributions to support the effort to rescue Palestine (though he

71. Mustafa al-Labbad, "Pressuring Tehran," *Al-Ahram Weekly*, 656 (2003).

72. The concept is based on the Qur'an (9:41): "Strive hard with your wealth and your lives," and (4:95–96), "Those believers who sit back are not equal to those who perform jihād in the Path of Allah with their wealth and their selves. Allah has favored those who perform jihād with their wealth and their selves by degrees over those who sit back."

73. Fatwās: Dr. Hussein Shihata, "Economic Jihād: A Legal Obligation and Religious Necessity," 10 July 2002, www.islamonline.net/fatwā/english/FatwāDisplay.asp?hFatwāID=70958.

stipulated that any acts of physical jihād should be coordinated with the Arab League).

Financially supporting armed jihād may be performed through a number of mechanisms, foremost of which is *zakāt*—the tithe that each Muslim must pay to the community for the orphans, widows, and poor within the community and for building religious institutions. (Originally, it was the duty of the Islamic ruler to allocate the zakāt to eight specific causes, including jihād and guarding the realm of Islam.)

The zakāt is, in essence, an Islamic income tax. In the absence of an Islamic ruler to allocate zakāt, the duty to support jihād has remained in force, at least in the eyes of many Muslims who accept it as such. If they are not inclined to perform jihād, donating money to support it is an acceptable substitute. Such support is equated with participating in jihād; not only is it a recommended act, but whereas actual participation in jihād may not be considered an individual duty by some scholars, supporting those who do wage jihād "for the cause of Allah" is a duty that a Muslim shirks on pain of inheriting hell.[74]

Many fatwās still include "charity for the sake of Allah (*sadaqa fi-sabīl Allah*)"—that is, for jihād—among the eight recipients of zakāt, which can be accomplished by allocating one-eighth of one's donation for the mujāhidūn. According to a fatwā issued by Sheikh Yousuf Qaradawi, if war is waged anywhere to free the occupied lands from the tyranny of kuffār, it is a case of "charity for the sake of Allah" and thus needs to be financed from the money of zakāt. The amount is to be decided based on the total assets of the charity, "the requirements of jihād, as well as the degree of the need of other potential recipients of charity."[75]

74. Fatwā: Dr. Hussein Shihata, "Economic Jihād" 10 July 2002, www.islamon line.net/fatwā/english/FatwāDisplay.asp?hFatwāID = 70958.

75. Sheikh Yousuf Qaradawi, "Spending Zakah Money on Jihād," 20 March 2003, www.islamonline.net/fatwā/english/FatwāDisplay.asp?hFatwāID = 18235.

Another form of funding derives from war booty, which fits into one of two main categories: *ghanīma*—booty that is taken during the battle and *fay'*—that is rounded up after the battle. According to traditional Islamic law, a fifth of all booty must be allocated to the needs of "Allah and the Prophet" (that is, public needs), the poor, orphans, and wayfarers. The rest must be divided among the mujāhidūn. The letter left by the leader of the September 11 terrorists, Muhammad 'Atta, recommends: "And if you slaughter then you take the booty of whom you killed, for this is a tradition of [the Prophet] peace be upon him."[76]

The issue of booty also touches on the question of whether stealing from kuffār in dār al-ḥarb is forbidden, as it is in dār al-Islām. The view supporting taking booty is based on the assumption that a state of jihād is in force vis-à-vis those countries, thus sanctioning acts (taking the spoils of war) that would otherwise be religiously prohibited. Accordingly, "Whatever the Muslims take in these wars—whether it is wealth, weapons, equipment, property, or whatever—in general belongs to the Muslims and it is permitted for them." This is not construed as stealing (which is forbidden in Islam) because stealing means taking property by "stealth and unlawfully from its proper place." The wealth of jihād (the spoils of war and the booty), however, are taken from the kuffār by a right that is rooted in shari'ah. The permission to take spoils of war is also rooted in the Qur'an: "So enjoy what you have gotten of booty in war, lawful and good" (al-Anfal 8:69) and in the tradition of the Prophet, who confiscated the wealth of the kuffār. The sin of stealing applies to property that is protected and is sacrosanct, but the property of the kuffār who are waging war against Islam is neither protected nor sacrosanct. Finally, taking booty is a means of "responding in kind," re-

---

76. Muhammad 'Atta's letter quoted in Reuven Paz, "Programmed Terrorists: An Analysis of the Letter Left Behind by the September 11 Hijackers," 13 December 2001, www.ict.org.il/articles/articledet.cfm?articleid-=419.

storing and giving back wealth that had been taken from the Muslims.[77]

Questions regarding the permissibility of robbing banks (either through breaking in or through bank fraud) are addressed in a number of fatwās. Most of the 'ulamā whose advice was sought were cautious not to sanction bank robbery in the West on the premise that no war is going on between those countries and the Muslims. In the case of Israel, however, stealing from banks is allowed because the money in those banks belongs to the enemy.[78] Scholars who forbid such behavior base their decisions on three principles: It presents a negative image of Islam and therefore is counterproductive to the mission of proselytizing for Islam, which is obligatory on every Muslim. It violates the terms of passage that allow Muslims to be in dār al-ḥarb and as such is treachery, which is forbidden. And because the wealth of the kuffār was obtained through treachery, it is in itself forbidden.[79]

Another form of economic jihād is boycotting the enemy's economy. Economic boycotts in the context of jihād call for Islamic justification and have been a source of conflicting fatwās. The tobacco fatwā issued in Iran (1892) by Ayatollah Shirazi was part of the struggle against British hegemony in the country. Economic boycotts are portrayed in the Qur'an both as a weapon of the pagans of Mecca against the new Muslim community and as a weapon of the Muslims against the pagans in Medina.

Fatwās declaring it a duty to boycott kuffār products or to refrain

77. Fatwā: Sheikh Muhammed Salih al-Munajjid. "Ḥukm Ghana'im al-Ma'arāk ilati yakhūdiha al-Muslimūn" (The law of booty in wars that the Muslims wage), n.d., http://222.islam-qa.com, question 7461.

78. Fatwā: Sheikh Faisal Malawi, "Robbing Jewish Banks," 20 April 2004, www.islamonline.net/fatwā/english/FatwāDisplay.asp?hFatwāID = 113492.

79. Fatwā: Sheikh Muhammad Al-Hanooti and Sheikh M. S. al-Munajjid, "Stealing from non-Muslims in the West," 1 September 2003, www.islamonline.net/fatwā/english/FatwāDisplay.asp?hFatwāID = 8619.

from employing kuffār are usually based on supporting the mujāhi-dūn, showing hostility toward the kuffār, and weakening their economic strength and hence their ability to wage a campaign against the Muslims. The rulings regarding Muslims who purchase American and Israeli products, however, fall short of delivering clear instructions. Knowing that a comprehensive boycott would be unfeasible, some prohibited buying such products with the reservation only "if there is no alternative"; others saw a boycott as a recommended act and thus did not brand those who ignored it as sinners.[80]

In November 2002, the Islamic Action Front (the Muslim Brotherhood of Jordan) held a conference of legal scholars that focused on the appropriate attitude to be taken toward the United States and Israel. The scholars agreed on a series of fatwās branding the United States as the enemy of Allah and the Muslim ummah because of its support for Israel and occupation of Muslim lands (Afghanistan), attacks on others (Libya, Sudan), and threatening of others (Iraq). The U.S. policy, as described in the fatwā, is a "crusader" policy, hostile to Islam and to Muslims. The exportation of American products to Muslim countries results in capital that supports that policy. Purchasing American products supports the enemy of the Muslims and is hence forbidden (*ḥarām*). Muslims were also warned that it is forbidden to sell "the American aggressor" a morsel of bread or a drop of water. [81]

80. Fatwās: Hussein Shiḥata, "Economic Jihād: A Legal Obligation and Religious Necessity," 10 July 2002, www.islamonline.net/fatwā/english/FatwāDisplay.a sp?hFatwāID = 70958; Sheikh Yousuf al-Qaradawi, "Boycotting Israeli and American Goods," 18 April 2004, www.islamonline.net/fatwā/english/FatwāDi splay.asp?hFatwāID = 30402;mt; Sheikh Faysal Mawlawi and Sheikh 'Abdel Khaliq Hasan Ash-Shareef, "Boycotting Products of the U.S. and Its Allies: Obligatory?" 22 March 2003, www.islamonline.net/fatwā/english/FatwāDisplay.asp?hFatwāID = 94 844;mt; Dr. as-Sayed Nuh, "Ulamā's Fatwā on Boycotting Israeli and American Products," 30 June 2003, www.islamonline.net/fatwā/english/FatwāDisplay .asp?hFatwāID = 69990; and many more.

81. *Al-Sabil* (Jordan) 11 November 2002, *Shihan* (Jordan), 9 November 2002, 15 November 2002.

Cease-fires and Treaties

Islamic law deals not only with the justification for jihād and the laws of engagement but also with the conditions for peace—treaty (*'ahd*), peace or reconciliation (*ṣulḥ*), and cease-fire (*hudnah*)—all of which apply to enemies who remain independent and are not subject to Islamic rule. Peace with those countries automatically applies a commensurate status on their citizens.[82]

No consensus existed among early scholars, however, regarding the permissible length of treaties or the possibility of extending them. The classic peace treaty—the Hudaibiyya Peace—which the Prophet concluded with the Quraish tribe in Mecca, was to last for approximately ten years, which was seen as the maximum period of truce possible with an enemy against whom a jihād was being waged. The precedent of the Hudaibiyya Treaty has become increasingly relevant in modern Islam, especially to peace treaties with kāfir countries with which Muslim countries have been at war. It was invoked, for example, by al-Azhar in Egypt to justify the Israeli–Egyptian Peace Treaty of 1979, and later by Yasser Arafat to downplay his acceptance of the Oslo Accords with Israel.

The Hudaybiya Treaty broke down when allies of the Quraish attacked allies of the Muslims, obliging the Muslims to attack Mecca and occupy it. That historical breakdown affects the way international relations are seen in contemporary fatwās, where attacks on "allies of the Muslims"—and certainly on Muslims—can serve as a casus belli, rendering treaties with the attacking side and their allies null and void, and obliging Muslims to renew the jihād.

What constitutes a treaty or peace in Islamic terms is widely debated because of the ramifications for relations with non-Muslims in non-Muslim countries. One position holds that all Muslim countries are in a state of treaty with all non-Muslim countries by virtue of bilateral diplomatic relations and multilateral membership in inter-

82. Peters, *Islam and Colonialism*, p. 32.

national organizations, foremost among them the United Nations. Accordingly, visas accorded to non-Muslims for Muslim countries must be viewed as writs of safe passage (aman) and honored. Moderate clerics have also used this claim to cite as criminal attacks on non-Muslims in Muslim countries. The radicals' counterargument is that the regimes that issue the visas are not Muslim, and therefore the treaties that they sign with kuffār countries are not valid, invalidating any writs they issue.

CHAPTER 7

Apostates and Apostate Rulers

MANY fatwās deal with the rulings of takfīr—the act of "heretication," or declaring individual Muslims (usually prominent intellectuals) as apostates (*murtadd*, pl. *murtaddūn*). These fatwās examine the criteria for defining such apostasy (*ridda, irtidād*) and the temporal and divine punishment for that crime. Whereas traditional Islam defined apostasy narrowly as denying the unity of Allah or the authenticity or finality of the Prophet Muhammad, modern fatwās consider a variety of "thought crimes" apostasy.

The two most obvious of these are converting to another religion and slandering the Prophet. One Shiite justification for punishing apostasy with death (apart from the punishments set in shari'ah itself) is comparing it to treason in Western civilization. The traitor leaves his community or sullies it, as does the apostate.[1] The second is slandering the Prophet, which is the form of apostasy Salman Rushdie is accused of. Most scholars agree that a person who commits that crime is an apostate and that "his blood may be shed and his property taken."

Along with these forms of apostasy, modern scholars cite "intel-

---

1. Fatwā: Sayyid Muhammad Rizvi, "Apostasy in Islam," May 1990, www.al-islam.org/short/apostacy.htm.

lectual apostasy." This term has come to signify the embracing of a wide variety of modern, reformist, or liberal ideas. The Egyptian Jihād and other radical groups have occasionally issued fatwās against such intellectuals as Nobel Prize-winner Naguib Mahfouz, and the writer Farag Fowda, among others. The late mufti of Saudi Arabia condemned as apostates those who claim that the earth is a sphere that revolves around the sun.[2] Many scholars, however, hesitate to declare such individuals as outright apostates, preferring to brand them as "hypocrites" (*munāfiqun*) whose fate is to inhabit the lowest rung of hell but who are not to be submitted to an earthly punishment.[3] In occasional fatwās, acts of intellectual apostasy have also been judged as apostasy pure and simple.

A number of fatwās discuss whether a Muslim's duty is to personally punish an apostate, including carrying out the death penalty. This discussion revolves around two main issues. The first is whether an apostate can repent and thus avert the sentence. Some scholars say that an apostate who was born a Muslim must be executed even if he repents, whereas one who has become a Muslim has the opportunity to repent, in which case he would not be executed. The second issue is whose duty or right it is to carry out the death penalty. Radical scholars have ruled that an apostate's blood and property are permitted to be taken and that there will be no retribution if a Muslim kills such a person. More moderate scholars have ruled that the death penalty is a prerogative of the Imām or leader of the commu-

2. Abdulaziz Bin Bāz, *Al-adillāh al-naqliyyah wal hissiyah 'ala jarayan al-shamsi wa-sukun al-arḍ wa imkan al-su'ud il al-kawakib* (The religious and empirical evidences that sun is moving and earth is still and the possibility of going to planets) (Medina: The Islamic University in Medina, 1975). "If the earth is rotating as they claim, the countries, the mountains, the trees, the rivers, and the oceans will have no bottom and the people will see the eastern countries move to the west and the western countries move to the east. . . . Those who claim that the earth is round and moving around the sun are apostates and their blood can be shed and their property can be taken in the name of God." Bin Bāz annulled the fatwā in 1985.

3. Fatwā: Yousuf Qaradawi, "Fatwā on Intellectual Apostasy," 24 March 2004, www.islamonline.net/fatwā/english/FatwāDisplay.asp?hFatwāID = 67088.

nity and that private executions may be a sin of "arrogating to one's self the rights of the Imām."[4]

Apostasy of a ruler (*takfīr*) is a particularly grave sin because it affects not only the sinner but causes other Muslims to become apostates. Until the late 1980s, the immediate enemy for most radical Islamic groups was not dār al-ḥarb and the kuffār but Muslim rulers and regimes that, in the eyes of those radical groups, had become apostate and thus forfeited the right to loyalty from Muslims.

The modern fathers of the takfīr doctrine were the Indian Abu Ilaa al-Mawdudi and the Egyptian Muslim Brotherhood leader Sayid Qutb. In the mid–twentieth century, Al-Mawdudi crafted the concept of the "modern jāhiliya." He claimed that the Muslim world was ignorant of the law of Allah that prevailed before Islam and therefore must be "re-Islamized." Qutb spent most of his life between 1954 and 1967 (when he was executed) in an Egyptian jail. There he developed a doctrine of jihād that promoted the struggle against those regimes within the Muslim world that had, in his view, become apostate and were leading Muslims astray. One of his ideological successors, 'Abd al-Salam Farag—a member of the Egyptian jihād movement responsible for assassinating President Anwar Sadat—disagreed with those who called for "focusing all the Islamic potential for liberation of the occupied Muslim holies from Zionism and colonialism." He argued that "this is not the right way to free those holies . . . the road for liberation of al-Qods [Jerusalem] is through the liberation of our land first from the kāfir regime because these regimes are the foundation of the presence of colonialism in the Muslim land."[5] A similar position was taken by Jordanian Sheikh Othman Abu Omar (Abu Katada): "Whereas there is no prohibition on fighting the kuffār before eliminating the apostate rulers, the very

4. Fatwā: Collective fatwā by a group of Islamic Researchers, "Apostasy: Definition and Ruling," 27 July 2003, www.islamonline.net/fatwā/english/FatwāDisplay.asp?hFatwaID=38268.

5. Mohamad 'Amarah, *Al-farīḍah al-Ghaiba—'Arḍ wa-ḥiwar wa-taqīīm* (The vanished duty: exposition and dialogue and assessment) (Cairo: Dar Thabet, 1982), p. 23.

existence of the latter, who draw their strength from the Jews and the Christians, weakens the potential of the Muslims to fight the kuffār."[6] Today, in almost every Muslim country (prominent among them Egypt, Algeria, Saudi Arabia, Afghanistan, and Pakistan), radical groups are waging a full-fledged jihād against their governments and leaders, whom they see as having lapsed into apostasy and leading Muslims astray.

This doctrine of jihād conflicts with the Islamic law prohibiting rebellion against Muslim rulers, about which the Qur'an is clear. Muslims are obliged to "obey Allah, the Prophet, and those in authority" and to make an oath of allegiance to the leader.[7] Declaring a leader a lapsed Muslim is not enough to override the prohibition against rebellion and justify jihād against him. Because war and civil strife between Muslims is unlawful in Islam, it may occur only when a true Muslim has become a kāfir.

The act of declaring a person (including a Muslim) a kāfir is a controversial one in Islam, for it is viewed with dread by most orthodox and moderate Muslims. Condemning someone as an infidel has its roots in the Qur'anic injunction 9:94 "Say not to anyone who offers you a salutation 'thou art not a believer.'" It was later stipulated that, if a Muslim calls another Muslim a heretic and the accused is not guilty of heresy, the accuser himself is a heretic.[8]

Thus, many fatwās that justify rebelling against Muslim leaders are in essence judgments of heresy. Because Islamic leaders' duties transcend those of common Muslims, the criteria for a judgment of

6. Fatwā: Abu Katada, members.nbci.com/_XMXM/bokatada/fatawa/000022.html.

7. Qur'an 4:59: "Whoever dies and did not make an oath of allegiance (to the Muslim leader) has died a death of jahiliyyah" (Narrated by Muslim, 1851); and "Whoever gives his oath of allegiance to a leader and gives him his hand and his heart, let him obey him as much as he can. If another one comes and disputes with him (for leadership), kill the second one" (Sahih Muslim, 1844).

8. "No man accuses another man of being a sinner, or of being a kāfir, but it reflects back on him if the other is not as he called him" (Bukhari, *Book of Ethics*; Book 78, ch. 44). The Hanafi school explicitly forbids takfīr.

heresy against them include special elements: annulling shari'ah or not allowing the practice of Islam; allowing that which God has forbidden and forbidding that which God has allowed; corruption on the face of the Earth; alliance with kuffār against Muslims (occasionally portrayed as "treason against the ummah," which is by definition also treason against God and against the Prophet); and allowing kuffār to occupy Muslim lands (that is, collaboration).

Since a judgment of heresy against a Muslim regime is a grave one, the leaders in those countries strive to convince jihād leaders to rescind such declarations. Egypt, for instance, successfully put pressure on the imprisoned leaders of the Egyptian Gama'ah Islamiyya to retract the judgment of heresy against the Egyptian regime and to renounce the use of terrorism inside Muslim countries.[9]

In contrast, the radical Saudi sheikh 'Abd al-Mun'im Mustafa Abu Halima (Abu Basir), issued a fatwā on July 5, 2003 regarding the possibility of a civil war and the breakdown of authority in Saudi Arabia. The sheikh accused the regime of according kuffār the same rights as Muslims and persecuting Islamic scholars and mujāhidūn (those two sins alone are enough to determine that the Saudi regime is "kāfir" and despotic). The sheikh went on to make a legal distinction between a general revolt (which he did not call for, as the necessary conditions of popular support are not yet in place), and personal action to eliminate the despotic regime, which the fatwā concludes is not forbidden.[10]

9. The Gama'ah Islamiyya in Egypt first published a retraction of their takfīr of the Egyptian regime in 1997 after an extensive crack-down on the group. In June, 2002, the imprisoned leaders began to provide interviews to the press condemning terrorism and denouncing takfīr. Eight leaders of the movement published a book in 2003 elaborating on the shari'ah aspects of their new attitude. Karam Muhammad Zuhdi, *Mubadarat waqf al-'unf—nazra shar'iya wa-ruya waq'iya* (The initiative for cessation of violence: a shari'ah and practical viewpoint) (Cairo: 2002).

10. Reuven Paz, "The March Goes On: Saudi Islamist Opposition Is Fighting Back," *Prism Series of Global Jihād*, 1, 7 (2003).

CHAPTER 8

Palestine, Afghanistan, and Iraq

A MUSLIM's exclusive identification with the ummah and the prohibition against his collaborating with kuffār against fellow Muslims have deep roots in Islam. The transnational identity of the ummah was one of the first political creations of the then new religion of Islam. As Islam gained ground, Muslims from a given tribe would have found conflict with his tribe socially and personally unbearable. Therefore, it became necessary to replace all prior tribal affiliation with a new affiliation to a trans-tribal ummah community, to command Muslims to be loyal to other Muslims and to distance themselves from kuffār.[1] Such identification with the ummah requires the same loyalty to Muslims from other countries, but may absolve Muslims of loyalty toward their own country when it contradicts their commitment to the ummah. This creates a dilemma that goes beyond that of the dual allegiance of an individual whose country of adoption is at war with his country of origin or with his coreligionists. Muslims living in a non-Muslim country face the problem of having to abide by the terms of citizenship in that country because violating them may reflect on other Muslims.

1. Qur'an (5:51): "O you who believe! Do not take the Jews and the Christians for friends; they are friends of each other; and whoever amongst you takes them for a friend, then surely he is one of them; surely Allah does not guide the unjust people."

There is a wide consensus among Islamic scholars that the Palestinians' armed struggle against Israel is a case of jihād becoming an individual duty for all capable Muslims, at least in Palestine.[2] Fatwās on this issue, free of the constraints regarding relations with the West, tend to range from calling for the complete mobilization of all Muslims for an active physical jihād against Israel, to moral and financial support of the jihād of the Palestinians.[3] Two similar but less prominent cases are the jihāds in Chechnya and Kashmir.[4]

The cases of Afghanistan and Iraq contain nearly all the elements of the legal reasoning involving the transnational identity of the ummah. The dilemma of whether or not to support the U.S. attack on Afghanistan is of particular interest, because it came immediately after the attacks of September 11, and though many Muslim scholars attempted at first to disassociate the teachings of Islam from the doctrines represented by the Taliban and bin Laden, the imperative to support Muslims who have been attacked by kuffār quickly gained precedence. Fatwās issued in response to the attacks on Afghanistan emphasized that "all Muslims are one entity" and that therefore an attack on one Muslim country is tantamount to an attack on all others.[5] Other justifications for supporting Taliban Afghanistan were the weakness of its people and that bin Laden's guilt had not been proven.[6]

Ostensibly, Iraq was a more complicated case. Even the most radi-

2. Fatwā: Sheikh Faysal Mawlawi, "Is It an Obligation to Join Jihād in Palestine?" 17 April 2004, www.islamonline.net/fatwā/english/FatwāDisplay.asp?hFatwāID = 82694; and Fatwā: Sheikh 'Abdul 'Aziz Ibn Baz, "Jihād in Palestine," 22 March 2004, www.islamonline.net/fatwā/english/FatwāDisplay.asp?hFatwāID = 44252.

3. Fatwā: Omar Bakri Muhammad, "Jihād Fatwā Against Israel," 2 October 2000, www.emergency.com/2000/fatwā2000.htm.

4. Fatwā: Sheikh Yousuf al-Qaradawi, "Fighting with the Mujahidin in Chechnya," 6 November 2000, www.islamonline.net/fatwā English/FatwāDisplay.asp?hFatwāID = 18231.

5. Fatwā: Islam Online Fatwā Committee, "Backing Fellow Afghans," 10 October 2001, www.islamonline.net/fatwā/english/FatwāDisplay.asp?hFatwāID = 51564.

6. Fatwā: Sheikh Yousuf Qaradawi, "Al-musharika fi-al-taḥaluf ma' Washinton ḍad Afghanistan Ḥaram" (The participation in the alliance with Washington against Afghanistan is forbidden), 16 September 2001.

cal Islamists had no illusions regarding the secular and oppressive nature of the Iraqi regime the United States set out to topple. The issue was not, therefore, Saddam Hussein's legitimacy as a Muslim ruler but the Islamic procedure for deposing such a ruler. The position of most 'ulamā was that the right to remove a ruler who failed in his duties toward his nation has been invested by Islam in the *ahl al-ḥall wa al-'aqd* (literally, the community of those who loosen and tie bonds—a nebulous concept referring to the leaders of the specific Muslim community), and that "the sword" should not be used to remove a dictator, because of the danger of the ensuing turmoil and because "fending off smaller harm must not result in creating a greater one."

This dilemma is compounded when a Muslim ruler is deposed with the help of kuffār, because it entails "disloyalty towards the Muslims" and "taking kuffār as allies," both of which are forbidden. This is especially true when the kāfir country is the United States, which has, many Muslims believe, ulterior motives, including taking the public property of Iraq, its natural resources, and its oil ("the property of the Muslims, which must be defended"); "exterminating the Palestinian cause" (a common code for seeking a peaceful settlement for the Israeli-Palestinian conflict) and "suffocating the Palestinian uprising" by exerting pressure on Syria to stop supporting the Palestinian Intifada; exerting the same pressure on Saudi Arabia to restrain radical 'ulamā and to create a secular, pro-American Kurdish state that would endanger the national security of (Muslim) Turkey and Iran.

Thus, the wars in Afghanistan and Iraq produced fatwās from scholars of all political shades concerning three ways to deal with the enemies of the Muslims.[7]

7. The most comprehensive of these were www.islamonline.net/fatwā/english/F atwāDisplay.asp?hFatwāID = 8619. Fatwā: The Islamic Research Academy of al-Azhar, "Jihād to Defend Iraq," 11 March 2003, www.islamonline.net/fatwā/english/F atwāDisplay.asp?hFatwāID = 94227; Fatwā: A group of muftis, "Seeking the U.S. Support to Topple Saddam," 15 December 2002, www.islamonline.net/fatwā/eng lish/FatwāDisplay.asp?hFatwāID = 75973; Fatwā: Sheikh Faisal Mawlawi, "Backing

The first concerns the individual duty of jihād. Is jihād incumbent on all Muslims in the wake of the American occupation, and how should it be implemented? The second involves active collaboration. May an individual Muslim serve in the military of a kāfir country engaged in a war against a Muslim country, provide it with intelligence (espionage), economic, material, or moral support (including serving in a government set up by a kāfir occupation), and may a Muslim ruler support an attack on Muslims? The third involves passive collaboration. May a Muslim request citizenship from a kāfir country involved in a war with Muslims? If he is a citizen or resident of such a country, may he obey antiterrorism acts that define various jihād organizations as terrorist and oblige him to report to the authorities on pain of being indicted as an accomplice?

The U.S campaign against Iraq saw a wave of individual and collective fatwās regarding the state of defensive jihād against any "alliance with the kuffār against the Muslims." These fatwās focused on three main arenas for jihād: inside Iraq proper, on neighboring countries with a U.S. military presence, and on U.S. interests around the world. Regarding attacks against U.S. forces in Iraq, the consensus quickly grew that U.S. and other foreign forces are legitimate targets because the U.S. presence in Iraq involved the occupation of a Muslim land by non-Muslims, rendering jihād an individual duty.

One of the first collective fatwās in this wave came from the Jordanian Muslim Brotherhood and its political arm, the Islamic Action Front, at the close of their Amman conference of November 2, 2002, which was attended by two hundred 'ulamā affiliated with the Broth-

the U.S.-Led War on Iraq to Remove 'Dictatorship,'" 23 March 2003, www .islamonline.net/fatwā/english/FatwāDisplay.asp?hFatwāID = 94720; Fatwā: A group of Muftis, "Attacking U.S. Bases in Arab Countries," 20 March 2003, www .islamonline.net/fatwā/english/FatwāDisplay.asp?hFatwāID = 94843; Fatwā: Faysal Mawlawi, "Attacking Iraq and Targeting the U.S. Interests," 15 March 2003, www.islamonline.net/fatwā/english/FatwāDisplay.asp?hFatwāID = 86869; and Fatwā: Sheikh Qaradawi, "Selling Food to the U.S. Troops Fighting in Iraq," 31 March 2003, www.islamonline.net/fatwā/english/FatwāDisplay.asp?hFatwāID = 95484.

erhood. On the eve of the Iraqi campaign, the Islamic Research Academy of al-Azhar issued a fatwā determining that an American attack on Iraq creates an individual duty of jihād for all Muslims.[8] Another wave of fatwās came in the wake of the fighting in Fallujah. On November 5, 2004, a group of twenty-six prominent Saudi Arabian 'ulamā issued a fatwā regarding the defensive jihād in Iraq.[9] Later that month, on November 18, 2004, another fatwā on Iraq was issued at a conference in Beirut by Sheikh Yousuf Qaradawi in his capacity as head of the International Association of Muslim Scholars (an association founded in London in June 2004).[10] All the above fatwās carried one basic message: Any attack on a Muslim country or occupation of such a country by kuffār automatically initiates a state of defensive jihād, which by definition is an individual duty.

The major rulings of these fatwās included several elements. First, jihād was declared an individual duty incumbent on every able Muslim. Any Muslim leader who attempts to suspend jihād will be guilty of "forbidding that which Allah has commanded." Second, prohibitions were placed on alliances with the United States and on cooperating with it by providing intelligence, airports, airspace, or seaports to U.S. forces. Third, boycotts were imposed on trade with the United States and on U.S. products. Fourth, bans were imposed on any Muslim support for military operations of the occupying forces, although such services as electricity, water, health, business, and public security to prevent looting and similar actions sometimes were permitted. (The Jordanian Muslim Brotherhood's fatwā prohibited even carrying water to Americans or Israelis.) Sheikh Qaradawi forbade support of any sort to the enemy, but he also proscribed attacks on the American-appointed Iraqi police, as long as they did not

---

8. Fatwā: The Islamic Research Academy, al-Azhar, "Jihād to Defend Iraq," 11 March 2003, www.islamonline.net/fatwā/english/FatwaDisplay.asp?hFatwāID = 94227.

9. Fatwā: translation on www.pbs.org/wgbh/pages/frontline/shows/saud/etc/fatwā.html.

10. On the IAMS fatwā, see *MEMRI, Special Dispatch Series 828* (December 2004), http://memri.org/bin/articles.cgi?Page = archives&Area = sd&ID = SP82804.

attack their own people. Fifth, the protection of Muslim noncombatants was required, while the Saudi fatwā ruled that "the blood and property of Muslims are inviolable." It added that it is in the interest of Islam and Muslims that oppressed and weak people who are not part of the conflict—especially those who are involved in humanitarian relief work, the media, or just earning their living—should not be harmed, "because the media are now focused on Iraq . . . [and] such acts may have negative consequences for Muslims." The Qaradawi fatwā adds that it is forbidden to take hostages and to threaten to execute them in an effort to pressure their governments, and that legitimate Western targets do not include women, children, or the elderly. This ruling, though, seemed to be contradicted by Qaradawi's rhetorical question, "Are there American civilians in Iraq?" which was construed as justifying attacks on all foreigners in Iraq.

The question remained, though, whether the American presence in neighboring countries, which facilitates U.S. military actions in Iraq, is a legitimate target. Some fatwās ruled that attacks on American bases in the gulf countries would cause direct conflicts with the regimes in those countries and that therefore such attacks should be limited. A fatwā issued by the deputy head of the European Council of Fatwā, Sheikh Faisal Mawlawi, dealt with the issue in another way: "If attacking these bases will not lead to internal strife (fasād), then the basic Islamic ruling is that they are aggressive troops and launching jihād against them is an individual obligation upon every Muslim who is able to do so. It is worth emphasizing that, in individual obligation, a Muslim does not need to seek the permission of the Imām or the Muslim ruler."[11]

The reasoning behind attacks on global U.S. interests is similar to that which justifies attacks on the American presence in countries neighboring Iraq. On this issue, however, most of the 'ulamā (includ-

---

11. Fatwā: Sheikh Faysal Mawlawi, "Attacking U.S. Bases in Arab Countries," 23 March 2003, www.islamonline.net/fatwā/english/FatwaDisplay.asp?hFatwaID = 9 4843.

ing radical ones) ruled that such attacks must be restricted to those who actually attack and kill Muslims; any other attack is only permitted in war conditions, which are determined by the Muslim ruler, meaning that only the Muslim ruler or Imām can decide issues relating to politics and the common good.

Immediately after 9/11, Muslim personnel serving in the U.S. army found themselves in a dilemma. It stood to reason that if extending material support to the United States was forbidden, then serving in its military was an even more grievous sin. One of the first fatwās to address those issues immediately after the attacks was signed by six Islamic scholars headed by Sheikh Qaradawi, which gave American Muslims a dispensation to continue to serve, albeit preferably not in combat positions.[12] This was a response to a question posed by the senior Muslim chaplain in the U.S. military, Muhammad Abdur-Rashid, regarding Muslim military personnel within the U.S. armed forces participating in the war operations and related efforts in Afghanistan and in other Muslim countries, either in combat or non-combat capacities.[13]

The beginning of the U.S. campaign in Afghanistan hardened the attitudes of some leading 'ulamā. A week after the campaign began, the new mufti of Egypt, Dr. 'Ali Gum'a, ruled in a fatwā that it is "forbidden for a Muslim to fight his brother, even if the guilt was proven," and that the Muslim soldier in the U.S. army must refrain from participating in the war; if he must participate, he is to serve in a non-combat function or submit his resignation. He is forbidden to

12. The scholars included Sheikh Yousuf Qaradawi, Judge Tariq al-Bishri (First Deputy President of the Council d'etat, Ret., Egypt), Dr. Muhammad S. al-Awa (Professor of Comparative Law and Shari'a, Egypt), Dr. Haytham al-Khayyat (Islamic Scholar, Syria), Mr. Fahmi Houaydi (Islamic Author and Columnist, Egypt), and Sheikh Taha Jabir al-Alwani (Chairman of the North America Fiqh Council). Fatwā: "Ulamā's Fatwās on American Muslims Participating in U.S. Military Campaign," 16 October 2001, www.islamonline.net/fatwā/english/FatwaDisplay.asp?hFatwaID=52014.

13. The shari'ah term used is *jā'iz*, the category of things which are permitted but are neither praiseworthy nor reprehensible.

kill a Muslim; if he kills one in error, he must pay reparations. If he kills one intentionally, he will be executed and suffer hellfire.[14]

Later fatwās took an even harsher stance. Whereas Dr. Gum'a's fatwā allowed the Muslim soldier in the kāfir army to serve as a noncombatant, even though such a role contributes to the war effort, the fatwā issued by a committee of clerics in the Jordanian Islamic Action Front declared that all those recruited by the enemy forces occupying Iraq or the security or military forces under their jurisdiction are "traitors against God, against His Prophet, and against the community of believers." The fatwā went on to declare any support for the enemy as "a declaration of war on God and His Prophet" and a form of apostasy (for which Islam reserves capital punishment).[15] Other fatwās ruled that "it is not permissible to work as a translator, or in any other field, for the occupying troops in Iraq unless your aim behind doing so is to obtain information about them in the interest of Muslim fighters."[16]

The intensified counterterrorism effort of the Western countries in the wake of the September 11 attacks generated a number of fatwās prohibiting Muslims from "spying" for the kuffār. One such fatwā, issued by Sheikh Omar Bakri Muhammad, the leader of the radical Muhajirun movement in the United Kingdom, ruled that "using intelligence services against Muslims or working for or cooperating with such bodies is prohibited according to the shari'ah," based on the ḥadīth: "Whoever earns and eats from exposing any secret of a Muslim, Allah will put fire in his mouth in *Jahannam* [hell], and whoever earns and clothes himself from exposing any se-

14. Fatwā: Dr. 'Ali Gum'a "Fighting the Muslims Is an Absolute Prohibition," 16 October 2001, www.islamonline.net/Arabic/contemporary/arts/2001/article10f.shtml.

15. Fatwās of Islamic Action Front, Amman, Jordan, 12 August, 2004.

16. Fatwā: A group of Muftis, "Being a Translator for Americans Troops in Iraq: Permissible?" 23 June 2004, www.islamonline.net/fatwā/english/FatwaDisplay.asp?hFatwaID=115811. The more hard-line rulings within the group were issued by the Palestinian Sheikh Ahmad Abu Halabiyah and the Egyptian Dr. 'Abdel-Fattah Idrees of the Palestinian and Egyptian religious establishments, respectively.

cret of a Muslim, Allah will clothe him with clothes of fire in Jahannam."[17] A number of fatwās warned Muslims in Iraq that providing any information on the Muslim mujāhidūn would be unlawful.[18] A fatwā issued by the Khilafah movement and the Shari'ah Court of the United Kingdom (a radical organization)—directed specifically against General Musharraf, the head of state of Pakistan—stipulates that Muslims who "ally themselves with the kuffār" by supplying them with weapons or praising them, formulating or signing contracts for them, or assisting them in their military action in any way have become "hostile apostates" (*murtadd ḥarbi*) and must be "killed, crucified, or have their hands and feet cut off on opposite sides."[19] Branding a Muslim as a hostile apostate is, according to this viewpoint, irreversible; once done, no amount of repentance can change the verdict.[20] Most 'ulamā who had not called for armed opposition to the existing Muslim regimes, however, remained wary of such judgments. A characteristic position was that of Sheikh Mawlawi, who said that committing sins, however grave they may be, cannot result in apostasy.[21]

The regimes created in Afghanistan and Iraq as a result of the oc-

17. Fatwā: Sheikh Omar Bakri Muhammad, "Regarding Being Part of the Intelligence," 6 June 2001, www.ci-ce-ct.com/Feature%20articles/13–10–2003.asp.; and Fatwā: Abu M'uadh Al-Makki, "The Islamic Verdict on Spies and Those Who Perform Espionage Against the Muslims," www.ci-ce-ct.com/Feature%20articles/13–10–2003 .asp.

18. Fatwā: Dr. 'Ali Jum'ah, Sheikh 'Abdus-Sattar F. Sa'eed of al-Azhar, and others, "Handing over Iraqi Fighters to the Americans," 31 December 2003, www.islamonline .net/fatwā/english/FatwāDisplay.asp?hFatwāID = 108856. A similar fatwā was issued later by Dr. Sano Koutoub Moustapha of Malaysia, "Assisting the Occupation in Killing or Capturing Iraqis," 3 April 2005, www.islamonline.net/fatwā/english/Fatw aDisplay.asp?hFatwāID = 102367.

19. Based on Qur'an (5:33).

20. Fatwā: Shari'ah Court of the U.K., 16 September 2001, against Pakistan President General Musharraf, USA in *MEMRI Inquiry and Analysis Series* 73, 24 October 2001, http://memri.org/bin/articles.cgi?Page = subjectts&Area = jihād&ID = IA7301#_edn42.

21. Fatwā: Faisal Mawlawi, "Assisting the U.S. Against Iraq: Apostasy?" 11 September 2003, www.islamonline.net/fatwā/english/FatwaDisplay.asp?hFatwaID = 86540.

cupation of those countries also posed challenges. A fatwā issued by
Egyptian sheikh Nabawi Muhammad El-'Eish ruled that the new
Iraqi council was "imposed upon the Iraqi people by the occupation
forces, to act as an ally to God's enemies" and that as such, any Arab
or Muslim country that lends it its support, or even deals with it,
should be boycotted.[22]

Some fatwās have questioned the legitimacy of obtaining citizenship in a kāfir country. Thus, the fatwā of Sheikh Ali abul-Hassan,
chairman of Egypt's Al-Azhar Fatwā Committee, ruled that obtaining or seeking to obtain U.S. nationality is forbidden, and branded
any person seeking to obtain U.S. nationality at a time when the
United States was acting against Muslims as an apostate allied with
the kāfir against the Muslim ummah and Islam.[23] In response to this
fatwā, the sheikh of al-Azhar, Muhammad Sayyed Tantawi, ruled
that acquiring American nationality is permitted, underlining the
distinction between citizenship and religion, on the assumption
that a Muslim holding a foreign nationality is seeking only to obtain
special privileges for his own interest and this is not violating shari'ah.[24]

The legal dilemma of citizenship in a non-Muslim country engaged in war with the Muslims goes beyond the area of formal citizenship, with a large body of fatwās dealing with the problems of
Muslims as minorities. Known as "the law of the minorities," (fiqh
al-'aqaliyyat) this area of shari'ah tends to be pragmatic and accom-
modating to the needs of Muslims in their adopted homelands. This
relatively new legal theory—promoted and led by Sheikh Taha Jabber
al-Alawani in the United States and Sheikh Yousuf Qaradawi in Europe—was formulated for Muslims residing outside Muslim countries to answer their unique problems as well as to help articulate
their identity. Showing an openness to the West, which is not seen

22. *Al-Ahram Weekly* (Egypt), 654, 4–10 September 2003.
23. www.islamonline.net/English/News/2002–1/14/article29.shtm.
24. Ibid.

as dār al-ḥarb but rather dār al-da'wah, public interest predominates over the bases of jurisprudence, and customary law is incorporated as a legitimate building block of shari'ah. This legal system, though it has the potential to generate tolerance toward the "other" among whom the Muslims reside, has not yet spread back to the heart of the Muslim world.

The enactment of antiterrorism legislation in many Western countries has created a severe legal dilemma for Muslims by broadening the scope of criminal culpability for aiding and abetting a wide range of activities related to terrorism, from transmitting instructions or documents to financial support, propaganda, or knowledge of terrorist activity. These Western definitions of criminality target key areas of the interaction between the mujāhidūn movements and the general Muslim public: fund raising (tithes [zakāt] for "the sake of Allah"), supportive infrastructure, and recruitment through religious institutions. It is criminalizing *knowledge* of terrorist activity, however, that places Muslims between Scylla and Charybdis. Respecting the law of the land would incriminate a Muslim under Islamic law for collaborating with kuffār against other Muslims, whereas remaining true to the Islamic code of loyalty to other Muslims would incriminate him according to the antiterrorism legislation.

A fatwā issued in January 2001, before the attacks of 9/11, by Sheikh Omar Bakri Muhammad, the leader of the Muhajirun, concerning the United Kingdom's Prevention of Terrorism Act 2000, clearly stipulates that "Muslim duties must not be affected by the new law of terrorism, whether it permits or forbids them from doing activities or from doing any actions . . . [as] all Muslims abide in all actions . . . by the command of Allah and his final Prophet, Muhammad, and no man made law must affect the brotherhood and relationship between Muslims globally, which is a cornerstone of their belief." A Muslim living in the U.K. who obeys the U.K. law, according to the sheikh, would be transgressing two major principles of

Islam: that "the Muslims are a single Brotherhood" (Qur'an 49:10), and that they have an obligation to show loyalty toward Muslims and to distance themselves from kuffār. Violating either of these principles is a grave sin and may even be considered apostasy, a crime punishable by death.[25]

25. Fatwā: Shari'ah Court of the U.K., Sheikh Omar Bakri Muhammad, "The Terrorism Act 2000," 19 January 2001. On al-walā wa-al-barā see also Khalid El-Gharib, "Al-Wala'u wa Al-bara' Revealed in Al-'Imran," Nida'ul Islam Magazine 20 (September—October 1997), www.islam.org.au/articles/20/tafseer1.htm.

CHAPTER 9

The War of the Fatwās

D
EMANDS from the western world and governments in the
Muslim world that Islamic scholars denounce jihādist
groups in Islamic terms meet with reluctance, for social,
political, and religious reasons. On the social level, denouncing acts of
terrorism is tempered by the tendency in Islam to search for common
ground and to avoid civil war among the ummah. On the political
level, those who condemn acts of violence against noncombatants frequently do not apply the condemnation to acts against Israel or
against the greater oppressor of the Muslims, the United States. On
the religious level, Sufi and modernist schools, which limit jihād to a
spiritual struggle or to winning converts by proselytizing, remain out of
the Islamic mainstream. Therefore, few Islamic scholars can disown
jihād as a military struggle or claim that it is foreign to the basic tenets
of Islam. Instead, it is the application of the principle of jihād and the
specific means used for fighting it that come under discussion.

The Muslim world is well aware of the significance of fatwās in
encouraging terrorism. In October 2004, a group of Muslim liberals,
rather than attempting reform within Islam, joined together to petition the secretary general of the United Nations to combat fatwās
that justified jihād. Their manifesto, published under the title "Fatwās Are a Primary Cause of Terrorism,"[1] called for establishing an

1. The promoters of the petition were the Jordanian writer and researcher Dr.
Shaker Al-Nabulsi, the Tunisian intellectual Al-'Afif Al-Akhdhar, and former Iraqi

international tribunal to prosecute individuals, groups, or entities involved, directly or indirectly, with fatwās issued by religious clerics urging Muslims to commit terrorist acts in the name of Islam. According to the manifesto, "By these fatwās all terrorists have died, or will die, fully convinced that they will immediately enter Paradise. Certain religious fatwās remain the pivotal cause of terrorist acts—fatwās that clothe such terrorist acts with legitimacy as being one of the sacred tenets of Muslim faith." In the same vein, former Kuwaiti minister of information Dr. Sa'd Bin Tefla complained that "despite the fact that bin Laden murdered thousands of innocents in the name of our religion and despite the damage that he has caused to Muslims everywhere . . . to this date not a single fatwā has been issued calling for the killing of bin Laden, on the pretext that bin Laden still proclaims 'there is no God other than Allah'" (i.e., is still a Muslim whose blood is inviolable).[2] The Kuwaiti minister's complaint points to a central issue: the harshest Islamic condemnation of terrorism would be to equate such acts with apostasy (i.e. to declare takfīr against the terrorist). Since apostasy is a cardinal sin that condemns its perpetrators to eternal hellfire and requires capital punishment for the apostate, condemnations of this type are few and far between.

Denouncing an act committed on the basis of a fatwā issued by a respected scholar not only condemns the terrorist but also implies a refutation of the legal and religious arguments of his spiritual mentor, suggesting anything from a mistaken reading of shari'ah to distorting the Qur'an (tahrīf, the fifth of the Jews and Christians who were said to have "corrupted" the scripture they received) to "forbidding that which Allah has permitted and permitting that which He has forbidden" (istihlāl)—an act which is tantamount to apostasy. The aversion in Islam to strife within the ranks of the commu-

---

Minister of Planning Dr. Jawad Hashem. www.elaph.com and www.metransparent.com.

2. *Al-Sharq al-Awsat*, 30 August 2004.

nity, and the ban on accusations of apostasy (takfīr) except in extreme circumstances, act as restraints. It is ironic that a religious mechanism meant to preclude accusations of apostasy, for fear that they would deteriorate into civil war, has become a tool in the hands of the radicals to deter criticism against them.

The positive side of popularizing the authority to issue fatwās is the lay Muslims' willingness to interpret Islam in contradiction to the radicals, and even to issue "lay fatwās" against them. One such bold challenge to the radical worldview is a fatwā issued by the Comisión Islámica de España on March 11, 2005, a year after the al-Qa'ida train bombings in Spain. Defined as "a fatwā against Osama bin Laden, al-Qa'ida, and those who claim to justify terrorism based on the Holy Qur'an," it focuses on the Qur'anic warning that "Allah does not love those who cause corruption (*mufsidūn*—causers of fasād)" (28:77), and the permission (not the obligation) that Allah has granted to respect non-Muslims who have not caused harm to Muslims: "Allah does not forbid you respecting and treating with justice those who have not fought you on account of your religion and have not expelled you from your homes" (60:8). This fatwā accuses bin Laden and other radical groups of istiḥlāl—falsifying and manipulating the sacred texts in order to "declare permitted that which Allah has declared forbidden, such as killing of [the] innocent and terrorist attacks." Such a sin renders its perpetrator an "infidel apostate who permits the forbidden" (*kāfir murtadd mustaḥil''*). Bin Laden, therefore, has become an apostate and should not be considered a Muslim. This—probably the strongest condemnation of radical ideology issued by a Muslim group using Islamic jurisprudential terminology—has not been backed up by any leading Islamic scholar in Spain or in the wider Muslim world.[3]

3. Fatwā: Comisión Islámica de España, "Fatua contra ben Laden, al Qaida y cuantos pretenden justificar el terrorismo fundamentándolo en el sagrado Corán o la Sunna del profeta Muhammad, Dios le bendiga y salve" (Fatwā against bin Laden, al-Qa'ida, and those who pretend to justify terrorism on the basis of the Holy Qur'an or the Sunnah of the Prophet Mohammad, may God bless and save him), Madrid, 11 March 2005.

Nevertheless, secular regimes in the Muslim world have supported voices of moderation among Islamic scholars, particularly when those voices counterbalance those of the radicals who oppose the regimes. One such example is Sheikh Ahmad Kuftaru of Syria, who headed the Naqshabandi Sufi order in Syria for decades and founded the Abu al-Nur Foundation with regime support. That foundation accepts the regime's predominance in all matters of state and proposes a modernist view of Islam (including a willingness to include all monotheistic religions as legitimate paths to God), in clear contrast to the Syrian Muslim Brotherhood (which also derives from the Naqshabandi order), headed by Sa'id Hawwa, 'Abd al-Fatah Abu Ghuddah, and others. It was, therefore, in the Syrian regime's interest to support the views of Sheikh Kuftaru.[4]

Jordan's late King Hussein also succeeded in channeling the Islamic element in his kingdom in a moderate direction. He was able to do this partly by virtue of his position as a descendant of the Prophet's family, and partly due to his alliance with the mainly East Bank Muslim Brotherhood, which had a vested interest in blocking the jihādi tendency in Jordan.[5] In a 1998 interview with Milton Viorst toward the end of his life, King Hussein pointed at the closing of the gates of ijtihad as a way of reconciling faith and present-day life. He also identified the defeat of the rationalist mu'tazila movement as having brought on the deterioration of Islam, which continues in modern times.[6] In addition, Hussein established the Aal al-Bayt Foundation, which propagates a moderate view of Islam and proper relations with the rest of the world. In the same spirit, his son, King Abdallah II, issued (in November 2004, during the Ramadan contemporaneous with the fatwā of twenty-six Saudi 'ulamā quoted

4. Itzhak Weismann, "Modern Sufi Attitudes Towards the West: Four Naqshabandi Cases," Unpublished manuscript.

5. Shmuel Bar, *The Muslim Brotherhood in Jordan* (Tel Aviv: Dayan Center, 1998), p. 5.

6. King Hussein interview with Milton Viorst, www.kinghussein.gov.jo/98_viorst.html.

above) a document (though not a formal fatwā) called the Amman Message (*Risalat 'Amman*).[7] Quoting relevant verses from the Qur'an, the message clarifies the principles of Islam that contradict acts of terrorism: respect for all human beings and the duty to act with latitude, rationality, tolerance, and the sanctity of human life. That message has become a key document of the Jordanian regime (posted prominently on the website of King Abdullah himself) but is a political, not a legal or religious, document.[8]

A few counter-fatwās have been issued by scholars, whose wording is significant because they try to circumvent the dilemmas posed by terrorism and relations between Islam and the West. One such document is a joint fatwā issued by Sheikh Hisham Kabbani, chairman of the Islamic Supreme Council of America, and Shiekh Seraj Hendriks, the mufti of Cape Town in the Republic of South Africa. The fatwā, which calls for interpreting the verses of the Qur'an on the basis of "the human situation and cultural milieu in which they were revealed and first applied," applies the principle of abrogation of verses (naskh). It accords *da'wah* (calling on the infidels to accept Islam) precedence over military jihād and defines a strong and righteous Muslim community as one "which performs right and forbids wrong." This is based on the claim that the Prophet himself spent thirteen years of his twenty-three-year mission building the Muslim community, rather than in jihād, and therefore the model of the Prophet that Muslims should follow is that of peace. It presents jihād as defensive only and links the "verses of the sword" to specific circumstances in which Muslims are attacked. Even then, jihād is not

7. www.kingabdullah.jo.

8. The follow-up conference in Amman (June, 2005) failed to reach a consensus of the 170 'ulamā from all branches of Islam and all schools of jurisprudence who participated; it restricted its efforts to achieving a declaration that only 'ulamā with authority may issue fatwās and that no Muslim may declare takfīr against another. In doing so, the organizers of the conference projected their sense of being on the defensive against the incitements of the radicals, their fatwās, and their declarations of takfīr. Instead of counterattacking, they called for a "ceasefire." *Al-Ghad* (Jordan), 30 June 2005: 1.

an individual duty but must be conducted by a Muslim leader (an imām). If there is none, one must be elected.[9]

Another such counter-fatwā was written by a Pakistani Islamic scholar, Mo'iz Ahmad, who responded to a question on the 1998 fatwā by bin Laden calling for jihād against Americans. The Pakistani's arguments include three main points. First, jihād is a collective duty and a fatwā on jihād should be addressed only to the collective representatives. No one else has the right or the authority to implement a fatwā. The verses quoted by bin Laden's fatwā to justify war against all kuffār are 9:5: "When the forbidden months are past, then fight and slay the pagans wherever ye find them, seize them, beleaguer them, and lie in wait for them in every stratagem"; 2:191: "And kill them wherever you find them and drive them out from where they drove you out since strife (fitna) is worse than war (qital)"; and 2:193: "And fight them until there is no more strife, and there prevail justice and faith in God." These make jihād a collective duty, dating from the period when a Muslim state existing in Medina had declared war against the pagans, who, in any case, were the polytheists of Banu Isma'il and not the People of the Book (Jews and Christians). Second, the verses are specific, not general. They are directed to the Companions of the Prophet in the specific circumstances that applied in that period. Third, verse 2:191 must be read as part and parcel of verse 2:190: "And fight in the way of God, against those who fight you, and do not exceed the limits, surely Allah does not love those who exceed the limits"; 2:192: "But if they desist then surely Allah is forgiving, merciful"; and the end of 2:193: "but if they desist [from fighting against you], then there shall be no war except against the oppressors."[10]

9. Fatwā: Shaykh Hisham Kabbani, Shaykh Seraj Hendricks, "Jihād: A Misunderstood Concept from Islam." Kabbani is chairman, Islamic Supreme Council of America; Hendricks is mufti, Cape Town, South Africa." www.sunnah.org/fiqh/jihād_judicial_ruling.htm.

10. Fatwā: Moiz Ahmad, 2 October 2001, www.understanding-islam.com/related/text.asp?type = question&qid = 1007#_f tn2. Ahmad is president of the Pakistani Al-Mawrid Institute of Islamic Research and Education.

The Pakistani counter-fatwā is conspicuous both in what it contains and what it lacks. The main argument against the radical interpretation—that verses must be read in both textual and historic contexts—is not accepted in the purist Hanbali school that is at the center of the legal and religious thought of the radicals and of most Saudi Arabian scholars. At best, the fatwā tries to refute the legal reasoning of bin Ladin's fatwā, but proclaims no judgment on its issuers or on those who act according to it.

One argument frequently used to justify Muslim cooperation with the West in the war on terrorism is that Islam has made "blood and property" inviolable (ḥarām) until the Day of Judgment (in fact, the quoted prohibition relates to blood and property of Muslims). He who violates that rule (that is, terrorists against whom the war is waged) is guilty of crimes of corruption or mischief (fasād), or destruction (hirābah). The individual Muslim—including a soldier—must struggle against such crimes, "enjoining good and preventing evil," and thus may perform civil or military duties. The determining factor, according to this fatwā, is the Muslim's intention. As long as he intends to apprehend the perpetrators of such crimes and those who have aided them, he need not be concerned with the consequences of the fighting that he is powerless to influence.

"Mischief" (fasād) and "destruction" (hirābah) are both grave crimes according to Islamic law, and the use of the terms in reference to terrorism warrants some reflection. According to Qur'an 5:33–34, concerning those who wage war against Allah and his Prophet and cause corruption on earth, both crimes are punishable by death, crucifixion, or exile. The legal definition of mischief involves crimes of piracy, highway robbery, and insurrection: "putting people in fear on the road, whether or not with a weapon, at night or day, in urban areas or in open spaces, in the palace of a caliph or a mosque, with or without accomplices, in the desert or in the village, in a large or small city, with one or more people . . . making people fear that they will be killed, or have money taken, or be raped." Destruction disrupts the order of society and is generally associated with dissent.

Punishment for the perpetrator of the mischief (*mufsid*) is jail; destruction is generally viewed as a crime left for the punishment of Allah. In any case, neither crime is on a scale warranting eternal perdition, nor does either preclude repentance.[11]

Moderate Islamic clerics' criticism of radicals focuses on Wahhabism per se. One such anti-Wahhabi cleric is Sheikh 'Abd al-Hadi Palazzi of Rome, who attacks two linchpins of radical reasoning: the definition of dār al-ḥarb and the logic that necessity can allow things that are essentially forbidden. Regarding dār al-ḥarb, he calls on the criterion of freedom of religion: As long as Muslims are free to practice their faith in Western countries (including Israel), these countries cannot be dār al-ḥarb. Regarding things that are forbidden, Palazzi argues that only a threat to the very existence of the Muslim community can allow such acts. Because neither a Western country nor Israel is threatening to destroy the Muslims, "necessity" cannot justify violations of the basic Islamic laws of war and prohibitions on harming "those whom Allah has forbidden to kill."[12]

The Sufi orders and their offshoots often assail the radical Wahhabi creed. In addition to the Syrian Sheikh Kuftaru of the Naqshabandi order mentioned above, another Sufi-oriented scholar who has aligned himself with secular Syria is the leader of the Ahbash (Ethiopians), Sheikh 'Abdallah ibn Muhammad ibn Yusuf al-Harari, who was closely connected to the Qadiriyya Sufi order in Jerusalem, Damascus, and Beirut. The Sufi and Ethiopian traditions of tolerance brought Sheikh 'Abdallah into conflict with the Wahhabi sheikhs. When the Ahbash movement spread to Southeast Asia, specifically the Indian subcontinent, it promulgated fatwās favoring coexistence between Muslims and practitioners of other religions. Sheikh 'Abdallah derives his legal thinking from the Ash'ariyya school (of the medieval Sheikh Abu al-Hasan al-Ash'ari, who died in 936 C.E., which endeavored to find a middle ground between rationalism and textual literalism) as reflected in his fatwās. The moderation of the

11. El Fadl, *Rebellion and Violence*, pp. 48, 54–56.
12. E-mail from Sheikh Palazzi to his newsgroup, 17 November 2004.

Ahbash in their attitude toward other religions is in sharp contrast to their violent stance against the Wahhabis, whom they define as kuffār and exclude from the ummah. Sheikh 'Abdallah ruled, in an extensive fatwā "exposing the misguided ways of Ahmad ibn Taymiyya," that the scholar who is revered by the radicals deviates from Islam on many issues and spreads heretical innovations. The Ahbash were, in turn, condemned by the Wahhabis as "a misguided group outside of the Islamic community" (*ahl al-Sunna wal-jama'a*) whose fatwās are not to be obeyed.[13]

Another critique of the radical worldview comes, ironically, from the extremely conservative 'ulamā circles that consider themselves true *salafis* (followers of the principles of the first generation of Muslims—*salaf*—the "predecessors"), in contrast to the "deviationist" Wahhabis. Attacking the radical Saudi Sheikhs Salman al-'Awda and Safar al-Hawali, and the doctrines of Sayid Qutb and Muhammad Surour, fathers of the jihād branch of the Muslim Brotherhood, the salafis describe the sheikhs as "those who promote setting up of parliaments and democratic elections, demonstrations in the streets, setting up of numerous party groups and organizations that split the unity of the ummah . . . [call for] open demonstrations in the Muslim lands . . . (which the Prophet and his Companions never did), call for taking part in open democratic elections (which the Prophet and his Companions never did), call for Marxist-style revolutions against the Muslim rulers (which the Companions never did), call for setting up of groups and societies and movements, each one of them claiming that it is upon the truth and is calling for unity whilst in reality they are causing more discord and more disunity which are as bad as (if not worse than) the sectarianism of the jurisprudent schools and the Sufi orders."[14] This group also criticizes the radicals

13. Mustafa Kabha and Haggai Erlich, "Al-Ahbash and Wahabiyya: Interpretations of Islam," Unpublished paper. See the website of the Ahbash, www.safeena .org.

14. Fatwā: Compiled by Abu Khadeejah Abdul Waheed as-Salafee (U.K.) according to http://www.islamonline.net/fatwā/english/FatwāDisplay.asp?hFatwāID = 8619 by Shaykh al-Albaanee (Jordan), Shaykh Muqbil ibn Waadiee (Yemen), Shaykh Ibn Baaz, Shaykh ibn Al-Uthaymeen, Shaykh Saaleh Fawzaan, Shaykh

for justifying prohibited deeds (such as suicide) on the basis of intent and believing that the fate of a Muslim who has committed a sin is deferred until the Day of Judgment.

Another attempt to refute the logic of jihād has been made by the Grand Ayatollah Imām Muhammad Shirazi, a Shiite scholar and marja'. Shirazi presents in fatwās and books a comprehensive analysis of "war, peace and nonviolence" according to his perception of Islam. His view of jihād is a traditional Shiite one based on the legitimacy of ijtihad. It uses both historical-contextual and holistic tools to justify moderate readings of the Qur'an, and it openly and unabashedly calls for bringing Islamic views of peace in line with those of the Western world. Some of the more salient elements in his rulings include interpreting the wars of the Prophet as wars of self-defense, thus undermining the claim that an offensive jihād is obliged by the sunnah of the Prophet; criticizing brutality in war as "exceeding the limits," which is forbidden; criticizing violence on the basis of public interest; defining not taking booty as a recommended act; prohibiting jihād in the absence of the Just Imām; total prohibition of suicide; rejecting the principle of reciprocity in retaliation; and emphasizing the Qur'an's prohibition against killing women, children, and other protected individuals.[15]

A number of fatwās issued in the wake of specific terrorist attacks walk a delicate line between the need to denounce such acts and the unity of the ummah. The theoretical framework of these fatwās is based on the growth of martyrdom attacks in the Israeli-Palestinian conflict, and the dissonance between the Western world's condemnation of those acts and their approval in much of the Muslim world.

The need to redefine Islamic jurisprudence toward acts of terror became acute after the September 11 attacks. Immediately following

---

Rabee ibn Haadee, Shaykh Ubayd al-Jaabiree, Shaykh Abdul-Maalik ar-Ramadhaanee, and Shaykh Abdul-Muhsin al-Abbaad (Saudi Arabia).

15. Muhammad Shirazi, "War, Peace, and Non-Violence: An Islamic Perspective," 2001, www.s-alshirazi.com/.

them, a number of fatwās and legal opinions addressed what had oc-
curred—was it an act of jihād (making the terrorists martyrs), or a
crime? If a crime, who were the culprits? The terrorists alone? Osama
bin Ladin? The Taliban? What were the precise transgression and
proper punishment (in this world and in the next)? What should be
the attitude of Muslim countries (particularly Pakistan) and Muslims as individuals (particularly Muslim military personnel in the
U.S. army) toward the impending U.S. attack on Afghanistan (a kāfir
country attacking a Muslim one), and the demand that terrorists be
apprehended and extradited (handing Muslims over to kuffār)?

Islamic establishments in Muslim countries and in the West issued a number of fatwās and statements of condemnation. Perhaps
the most coherent of these was the fatwā issued by the head of the
Supreme Council of 'Ulamā of Saudi Arabia, Sheikh Salih bin
Muhammed al-Lahiddan. In his fatwā of September 14, 2001, he
enumerates a list of relevant sins that are all forbidden in Islam: injustice among humans; aggression against those who have committed no crime; killing innocent people, the weak, infants, women, and
the elderly; destroying property; mischief (corruption); and laying
waste to the land. The fatwā stopped short, however, of specifying
the divine punishment for those who had planned and perpetrated
the attacks of 9/11. Rather, it defined those who commit such crimes
as "the worst of people" and said that no Islamic scholar could con-
done such acts.[16]

Another response was that of Sheikh Yousuf Qaradawi (September 12, 2001), whose fatwā denied the attacks' legitimacy by elaborating on the Islamic "respect for the human soul and prohibition on
harming it." He held that Islam does not permit the indiscriminate
killing of the innocent along with the guilty because "no one may
carry the burden of the other." Therefore, if the act was perpetrated
by a Muslim, "we condemn and incriminate him in the name of our

16. The fatwā is translated on the website of the Islamic Center, Washington,
D.C., www.theislamiccenter.com/AlNur.5.02/judicial.html.

religion and our law and he deserves the lawful deterrent punishment." Though the killing of people in general was defined as "one of the graver sins," the act was not declared a sin of heresy but rather a crime deserving legal (that is, temporal) punishment. Moreover, the fatwā made no reference to punishment in the afterlife for those who perpetrated the attack or their dispatchers.[17]

On September 17, 2001, a week after the attacks, the mufti of Saudi Arabia, Sheikh 'Abd al-'Aziz Aal al-Sheikh, issued a fatwā describing the attacks as "actions that shari'ah does not sanction" and "not from this religion." Basing his ruling on the principle that "no person can bear the burden of another" (Qur'an 6:164), he saw hijacking planes and mass murder as "injustice, oppression, and spreading of corruption on earth," which even hatred does not justify. A similar position, taken by Sheikh Salih al-Suhaymee (October 18, 2001), put such acts in the category of illegal sexual acts, disrespect for parents, polytheism, and killing without reason. Because Allah has forbidden killing non-Muslims who have a treaty with Muslims, women, children, the elderly, and monks, as well as cutting down trees (destruction of fruit-bearing property), the attacks of September 11 were "not permissible" (ghayr ja'iz)—though not explicitly prohibited.[18] The jailed leader of the Egyptian Gama'ah Islamiyah, Sheikh Karam Zuhdi, based the illegality of the 9/11 attacks on the prohibition in Islam on killing merchants (i.e., caravans, etc., in the seventh century) because merchants, as well as Muslims, were killed in the attacks.[19]

The various levels of prohibited acts as defined by Islamic law are of particular importance, because the terms used to describe them express not only the degree of denunciation of such acts but also the

17. Fatwā: Sheikh Yousuf al-Qaradawi and others, 12 September, 2001.

18. Fatwā: Sheikh Saalih as-Suhaymee, 18 October 2001, www.fatwā-online. com/news/0011018.htm. The rationale for the mention of the categories of women and children and fruit trees is commonly that all three can bring benefit to the Muslims.

19. Karam Zuhdi, Al-mussawar (Egypt), 21 June 2002: 1.

punishments, temporal and divine, that should or will be meted out to the transgressor. The classic categories of duties and prohibitions are frequently circumvented, and equivocal terminology is used. In the parlance of denunciations of terrorism, we find terms such as "a forbidden criminal deed" (*'amal ijrami munkar*), "reprehensible" (*makrūh*), grave transgressions (*fisq*), great crimes (*kabāīr*), "transgressing the limits," "going to the extreme" (*ghulū*), "allowing that which is forbidden" (*istiḥlāl*), "corruption upon earth" (*fasād 'ala al-arḍ*), "strife" (fitnah), "great harm and inconvenience caused to the innocent," "a mistake, ignorance and falsehood," a "grave criminal act that Islam does not approve of and no one should applaud," "acts that the total effect of which none can comprehend except Allah," and, simply, "not of Islam." The Islamic basis for prohibiting attacks on civilians are the Qur'anic verses: "No person shall bear the burden of another" (6:164), "Whoever slays a soul, unless it be for manslaughter or for mischief in the land, it is as though he slew all men" (5:32), and "Fight for the sake of Allah against those who fight against you, but begin not hostilities" (2:190). Thus, the terrorists may be dubbed criminals or misguided. Rarely—and in none of the fatwās of prominent mainstream 'ulamā—have they been condemned as apostates or heretics.

Another watershed event that prompted religious authorities to issue counter-fatwās was a series of attacks launched against non-Muslims in the kingdom of Saudi Arabia. On February 7, 2003, the Council of 'Ulamā in Saudi Arabia issued a fatwā forbidding attacks on non-Muslims anywhere in the world, for "the shedding of the innocent blood and the bombing of buildings and ships and the destruction of public and private installations is a criminal act against Islam," and it is a crime to randomly judge people as infidels and target them. The perpetrators of such acts are accused of "holding deviant beliefs and misleading ideologies."

In the wake of a series of terrorist attacks in Saudi Arabia (May 13, 2004), seventeen Saudi sheikhs—led by the head of the Supreme 'Ulamā Council, 'Abdul-Azeez bin Abdullaah bin Muhammad Al ash-Shaykh—issued a fatwā condemning them.[20] This cautious fatwā stopped short of describing the attacks as warranting far-reaching religious sanctions against the perpetrators but defined the attacks as "a disgraceful crime" (*jarm shani'*—a general negative description that does not carry any particular Islamic connotation), a great "*munkar*" (reprehensible act), and a type of "corruption upon earth."

More significantly, a group of opposition 'ulamā[21] issued a fatwā that follows the establishment fatwās in defining the attacks as "a disgraceful crime," because it is prohibited to harm any "immune soul," whether it be a Muslim, a non-Muslim who has a pact with the Muslims, a non-Muslim with a writ of passage or visa, or a non-Muslim living in a Muslim country (dhimmi).

The bombing of a Bali nightclub also drew reactions from prominent scholars. In contrast to the attacks on New York and Washington, the attack in Bali took place within a Muslim country against visiting non-Muslims. The scholars' condemnations focused on the attacks targeting tourists, who, by virtue of their having entered a Muslim country legally, should be protected. The attack on property was also condemned, as Islam forbids destroying property and harming honor in jihād; therefore, these acts were to be considered acts of "corruption in the land."

In the wake of the July, 2005 attacks in London, the Fiqh Council of North America issued a fatwā against terrorism (July 28, 2005). The fatwā declares that "Islam strictly condemns religious extremism and the use of violence against innocent lives. . . . There is no justification in Islam for extremism or terrorism. Targeting civilians' life and property through suicide bombings or any other method of attack is harām—forbidden—and those who commit these barbaric

20. The fatwā was issued on May 14. For an English version, see www.tazkiyah .org/content/riyaadh.php.

21. Including Sheikh 'Abd al-Rahman al-Burak, Sheikh 'Abdallah al-Jibrin, Sheikh Safar al-Hawali, Sheikh Salman al-'Awdah, Sheikh 'Abdallah al-Tuweijari, and Sheikh Nasser al-Omar.

acts are criminals, not "martyrs." The fatwā concludes that all acts of terrorism targeting civilians are ḥarām (forbidden) in Islam; it is ḥarām for a Muslim to cooperate with any individual or group that is involved in any act of terrorism or violence; it is the civic and religious duty of Muslims to cooperate with law enforcement authorities to protect the lives of all civilians.

The ISNA fatwā powerfully expresses the difficulty faced by mainstream Muslims who endeavor, on one hand, to condemn terrorism in terms understood by Western ears, and, on the other, to remain true to the constraints of Islam. It does not define the "terrorism" (a concept not defined by Islamic law) that they condemn. It refers, instead, to "civilians"—a concept not recognized by the Islamic law of jihād, and brands the terrorists as "criminals," which is a category of civil, not religious, transgression. The verses it invokes to condemn terrorism—"For this reason did We prescribe to the children of Israel that whoever slays a soul, unless it be for manslaughter or for mischief in the land, it is as though he slew all men" (5:32), and, "Let there arise from among you a band of people who invite to righteousness, and enjoin good and forbid evil" (3:104)—leave room for interpretation. Since the radicals claim that their actions are in response to "mischief" (fasād), and are a form of "enjoining good and forbidding evil," the ISNA fatwā is not a clear-cut condemnation of terrorism. The crimes of the terrorists, according to all these fatwās, are not acts of heresy or even tantamount to heresy.[22] They are crimes derived from four main violations: of the sanctity of the land of the Muslims, of the prohibition against harming any protected person without reason, of the prohibition against corruption upon earth, and of the prohibition against destruction of protected property.

22. www.cair-net.org/includes/Anti-TerrorList.pdf.

Conclusion

S INCE September 11, 2001, it has been said often that the West is fighting a war of ideas that cannot be won through military action alone. Indeed, it may turn out to be one of the longer wars of human history. The strategists of this war, however, have yet to identify the ideas on either side of the divide. Is it liberal democracy versus totalitarianism, or Western enlightenment versus Muslim obscurantism? Or liberal peace-loving forces, including mainstream or moderate Islam, versus fundamentalist and radical Islam? Or should the ideas pitched against each other be, in the end, two Muslim worldviews—on one side the confrontational and violent one of the radicals, on the other, a Muslim reformism or traditional conservatism, which, while it may not subscribe to the ideals of Jeffersonian democracy, does not seek to destroy those who do?

This war of ideas is a religious war. Whether or not the West sees it as such, it has been so defined by the adversary. Attempts to attribute Islamist terrorism to political and economic circumstances alone create the false hope that the problem can be dealt with by political and economic reforms. Islamist terrorism derives legitimacy and justification from Islamic mores and legal thought, and any attempt to deal with it divorced from its intellectual, cultural, religious, and legal fountainhead will be in vain. The belief that the conflict can be resolved through primarily military means (proving to "the Muslims" that conflict with the West is counterproductive to their collective interests) is also an illusion: The ideology that has taken root in radical Islam confounds classic military theories of deterrence. If an act of jihād is, by definition, an act of faith in Allah, by fighting a weaker or equal enemy the Muslim is relying on his own strength, not on Allah. By entering the fray against all odds, the mujāhid is proving his utter faith in Allah and will be rewarded accordingly.

The role of radical 'ulamā and their fatwās in legitimizing terrorism is a pivotal one in the social and political legitimization of terrorism and in the motivation of its foot soldiers. Whether the authors of the fatwās analyzed here are politically motivated or genuinely feel themselves moved by divine hand, their impact is incontestable. Not mere cynical political manifestos aimed at motivating the already converted followers of radical Islamic ideology, they play a pivotal role in convincing believing Muslims through religious and legal arguments to adopt the path of jihād. For many recipients, these fatwās represent a road map to the "straight path," which is "fixed by a system of divine laws that trump any moral considerations or ethical values."[1]

The fatwās commanding terror must be countered by a clear opposing consensus of mainstream 'ulamā. Such a consensus does not yet exist. On the issues relating to Islamic terror, the mainstream 'ulamā are silent, and for many of their followers silence equals consent. This is due not only to the absence of a formal mechanism to achieve such a consensus (such as an Islamic Supreme Court) but also to the deference that mainstream 'ulamā pay to the radicals, seeing them as the quintessential believers, as well as competing with them for the same constituency. Such deference exists in other revelation-based religions, but it is strengthened in Islam by the explicit prohibition on accusations of apostasy, the aversion to the introduction of strife and turmoil within Islam, and by the sense of many establishment 'ulamā (disparagingly called *'ulamā al-Sultan*—

1. Khaled Abou El Fadl, Tariq Ali, Milton Viorst, and John Esposito, *The Place of Tolerance in Islam* (Boston: Beacon Press, 2002), p. 4.

the 'ulamā of the regime) that they are compromised by their alliance with corrupt secular regimes and that popular sentiment is on the side of the radicals. There is no doubt that many scholars, and certainly many lay Muslims, do not personally subscribe to the radical narrative. They have not as yet, however, proposed an alternative. It is on the home field of this presumed silent majority that the main battle needs to take place, and as long as the silent majority does not enter the fray, the battle cannot be won.

The popularization of Islamic jurisprudence that resulted in the issuing of fatwās by lower-level 'ulamā, many of them lacking the requisite Islamic education to be considered muftis, may have its positive side. Once the monopoly on interpretation has been broken, the road may be open for other interpretations and ijtihād, not only from the radical side but also on the part of moderates and liberals. The fatwā issued by a group of lay Muslims in Spain (see chapter 9) may be a harbinger of this trend.

The lack of resolve on the part of Islamic establishments and regimes of the Middle East to confront the issue is evident. When the basic interests of these regimes were in danger, they proved their ability to coerce religious establishments and even radical sheikhs to rule in a way commensurate with their needs. Few of them, however, show any inclination to join a global (that is, infidel) war against radical Islamic ideology. Muslim regimes also hesitate to crack down on the religious dimension of radical Islam; they satisfy themselves with dealing with the political violence alone. They trade tolerance of jihād for local calm and lose ground to radicals in their societies. Hence, the prospect of enlisting Middle Eastern allies in the struggle against Islamic radicalism is bleak. Under these conditions, it will be difficult to stop young Muslims in the West from converting the ideas of radicalism emanating from the "safe houses" of the Middle East. Even those who are not in direct contact with Middle Eastern sources of inspiration may absorb the ideology by interacting with other Muslims in schools and on the Internet.

Meanwhile, the call for reform—albeit a noble and worthy long-term goal that would help put Islam in harmony with mainstream global civilization—seems, for the time being, a chimera. The very demand for reform is widely perceived in the Muslim world as another form of Western intervention within Islam, assailing the religion of Islam directly instead of merely corrupting the Muslim society and family. Furthermore, religions are naturally conservative and slow to change; when they do, it is the result of internal processes. The history of religious reform indicates that it can result from top-down revolutions (where there exists a supreme spiritual leader such as a pope, high priest, or Shiite Imām); from an accepted mechanism of scholarly consensus (for example, the Talmud or the consensus of the ijtihād in early Islam); from internal social revolution (similar to Luther's Protestantism); from the trauma of a collective calamity (such as the destruction of both Holy Temples in Judaism); and from gradual development over the ages, subject to reactionary backlashes of purists. Until now, Sunni Islam has known none of the first four catalysts of reform, and the last has not been thorough enough to completely purge mainstream Islam of radical concepts. Ironically, the modern revolution in Shiite Islam led by Ayatollah Khomeini has been in the direction of radicalization. Nevertheless, the school of "law of the minorities" that looks for practical solutions for Muslims living in the West, and the quietest traditions of Shi'ah Islam, which have survived not only in Najaf but also in Qom, can serve as potential forces for restraining radical interpretations.

Stemming the tide of radicalism within Muslim society cannot wait for reform or revolution in Islam. It is a higher priority than the need to modernize medieval dogmas of society and economics. The answer may be found in the dormant "tool box" of mainstream orthodox Islam, which includes religious concepts that can be revived to strike a new balance between the mainstream and the radicals. On the ideological plane, this includes reviving ijtihād, which would allow the verses of the Qur'an to be interpreted according to the "reasons for revelation," which may legitimately contradict the radical interpretation of those divine injunctions. Restricting a problematic verse to particular circumstances would diminish its radical potential. This common tool of reformers has its roots in medieval Islamic jurisprudence. The diversity of interpretations and rulings of the early jurists of Islam provide a basis whereby modern traditionalists can choose interpretations compatible with contemporary circumstances without explicitly resorting to reform. However, use of this method for delegitimizing acts of terrorism calls for incriminating branding the terrorists as heretics (takfīr), and in sowing internal strife them and corruption (fasād), and destruction (hirābah). Doing so would cause the legitimacy of financially supporting the terrorist movements to be lost, and the intimate link between the orthodox and the radicals to be severed.

In practical terms, what is needed is a clear disengagement from any justification of violence and a willingness to clearly demarcate the borders between the mainstream and the radicals. Such a disengagement cannot be accomplished by declarations of condemnation. Rather, it requires clear and binding fatwās that undermine the radical narrative. These may include fatwās declaring that not only does no personal duty of jihād exist but that justifying jihād under the present circumstances is a willful distortion of the roots of Islam and is, thus, an act of heresy. Such fatwās should determine that physical, moral, or financial support for terrorism is prohibited (haram) and condemn its perpetrators to eternal hellfire. Indeed, for every fatwā that promises Paradise to those who engage in jihād, a counter-fatwā should threaten hellfire.

Paradoxically, to combat the radical trend in Islam, what is needed is a "war of apostasy" of the orthodox against the radicals. To the Western ear, this may sound medieval and incompatible with principles of freedom of religion and expression. It is even dangerous in the context of Islamic law, because an apostate may be killed and the killer absolved. The fear of fomenting internal turmoil inherent in such an attitude, however, has cowed Muslim moderates and restrained them from an all-out condemnation of the jihād movement.

In the absence of an Islamic reformation, a war of apostasy may be the only way to combat the jihād movement within Islam.

In the meantime, the Western political and legal arsenal needs to adapt itself to the reality of a religious war. This may call for reinterpreting the boundaries of freedom of religion so as to include prohibiting certain acts and statements, even if based on scriptures, and redefining the principle of personal criminal culpability to indict religious leaders for the acts of their flock as a result of their spiritual influence. Such modifications may put pressure on basic principles of Western democracy. Under the circumstances, it may be the lesser evil.

Afterword

SINCE THE SEPTEMBER 11 ATTACKS, much attention has been paid in the West to the justification of terror by Islamic scholars. Most in the West, however, continue to see the positions of radical scholars as an aberration, a drastic departure from the main body of Islamic jurisprudence. This book grew out of the need to bring into focus the mainstream tenets and fundamental theological assumptions that nourish the radical positions and confer upon them wide legitimacy. That need has not abated.

On the 14th of September 2006, the government-controlled Saudi Arabian newspaper *al-Watan* (the Homeland) conducted a poll of senior Sunni clerics from Saudi Arabia, Egypt, Jordan, Syria, and Yemen on the statement of the former Iranian President Muhammad Khatami at Harvard University that the perpetrators of the 9/11 attacks are not in Paradise, but rather in "Hellfire." Approaching the issue from the vantage point of Sunni jurisprudence, the participants in the poll were largely in agreement: it is not permitted to make a judgment because that would contradict the belief of the Sunni, or those who hold on to the Sunna (the traditional portion of Muslim law, based on the words and acts of Muhammad, and preserved in the traditional literature). No true Muslim may presume to know whether another Muslim has been consigned to Paradise or to Hell since such a judgment is the sole prerogative of God. The Qur'an specifies certain persons who are in Paradise and others who are in

Hell; all others are left to God's judgment. Anyone who claims otherwise is a "deceiver" who strays from Islam.

The *al-Watan* symposium was not surprising. It faithfully reflected many of the arguments I found in the hundreds of pages of fatwas I collected over the years and which formed the basis of this book. Like the relatively small number of more moderate scholars who immediately condemned the attacks, some of the *al-Watan* respondents described them as "crimes"—"corruption (*fasad*) on earth" and "destruction" (*Hiraba*), because they were perpetrated against people who cannot be held accountable for the crimes of their governments. Others hedged, claiming that the acts damaged, or at least did not serve, the interests of the Muslim nation (*umma*). However, even the most moderate of sheikhs did not go further than to justify the punishment of such people in this world (according to the Qur'an—to be crucified and have their opposite arms and legs amputated). None would take the decisive step of declaring that such "criminals" will not be considered by God to be martyrs but rather will burn in eternal Hellfire. True to the fundamentals of Islam, all agreed that actions alone cannot be a criterion for claiming that those who were responsible are damned. Only Allah knows the hearts of the believers and He judges them also according to their intentions.

Since the publication of *Warrant for Terror*, I have continued to comb Islamic publications in vain for an unambiguous legal declaration that those who perform acts of terrorism against innocents have "left the community of Islam" by becoming "apostates" and should be sentenced to Hell. The few voices that were heard in the wake of the attacks and called for a reassessment or reform inside Islam have all but died down or have been stifled by more vocal and violent opponents. The official "war of ideas," launched by the United States was aimed at the radicals, but hampered by political correctness, it has not dared to address the philosophical and theological roots of the radical world view in widely practiced versions of Islam. The problem has been compounded by attempts in some Western political and law enforcement bureaucracies to appease mainstream Islam by obscuring the core issues through the redescription of jihadist terror as "religiously motivated acts of violence."

The theologically based jurisprudence described in this book remains in force. An interesting addition to the theological aspect was added by none other than Pope Benedict XVI in his 2006 "Regensburg Address." The Pope addressed the absence, in Islam, of the theological assumption that God acts "rationally" and restricts his omnipotence so as to do only "good," allowing humans – through their own God-given reason – the capacity to distinguish between good and evil.

As I argued in *Warrant for Terror*, that Islam denies Man this capacity is the crux of the matter: The Qur'anic version of the fall from Eden recounts how Adam ate from a tree that God commanded him not to touch, and was punished for his disobedience. But the tree was not the "Tree of Knowledge of Good and Evil." Hence, the Islamic Adam and his descendants lacked essential moral knowledge. This demotion of the human capacity to reason morally was compounded in the fourteenth century by the defeat and condemnation as heretics of the Mu'tazilite school, which held that it was possible to reason about God's will and ways. The debate whether God is rational and whether humans should presume to determine His will took place in all three great monotheistic religions. In Christianity and Judaism, the rationalists (Maimonides and Aquinas) carried the day. In Islam they did not. Consequently, contemporary Muslim scholars lack the theological infrastructure to claim that they know that acts of terror are anathema to God's will and that their perpetrators are damned to Hell.

The struggle against jihadist terrorism must begin, therefore, inside mainstream Islam. Until the mainstream scholars of the Muslim world muster legitimate theological arguments that damn those who murder innocents to Hellfire, the West will continue to wage the war on terror lacking a crucial ally in the war of ideas.

Glossary of Selected Terms

ahl al-ḥall wa al-'aqd: those who loosen and bind—the elites of the community who are trusted with decision making for the community.

ahl al-kitab: people of the book—a reference to Jews, Christians and Zoroastrians (*Majūs*). A member of one of these communities is a *kitabi* (pl. *kitabiyun*).

ahl al-qitāl: People of the fighting—combatants, those who the *mujāhid* is obliged to kill during the fighting.

al-yāwm al-akhīr: The last day (Day of Judgment).

amīr: commander: military commander of *mujāhidūn*.

Amīr al-Mu'minīn: commander of the faithful.

amr bil-ma'rūf wal-nahi 'an al-munkar: commanding that which is good and prohibiting that which is evil.

'aqīdah: faith.

arkān (sing. *rakan*): the five pillars of Islam (declaration of faith, almsgiving, Haj, Ramadan, Prayer).

'ars al-shahādah: the marriage with martyrdom. Also *'ars al-mawt*—the marriage with death. The ideal of falling as a martyr.

asbāb al-nuzūl: reasons (circumstances) of revelation—a technique for interpretation of the Qur'an according to the circumstances in which a certain verse was revealed. Similar to *takhsīs*—linking a verse to specific issues.

baghi: rebellion.

bay'a: oath of allegiance to the Caliph of Amir.

bid'a: innovation. Customs not rooted in Qur'an and *Sunna*.

dār al-'ahd: House of Treaty—a land that has concluded a treaty with the Muslims.

dār al-Islām: the House of Islam—all lands that are under Islamic rule.

dār al-ḥarb: the House of War—all lands in which Islam is not the law.

dār al-kufr Ghair ḥarb: House of Heresy, a land that is *not* at war with the Muslims.

dār al-ṣulh: House of Peace—a land that has concluded a peace treaty with the Muslims.

dār al-ḥiyād: House of Neutrality—a specific category for Ethiopia by virtue of the Ethiopians having given refuge to the early Muslims during the first *hijra*.

Daʿwah: the call to Islam. By Islamic law of war, it must precede *jihād*.

dawla: state.

dhimmi: members of ahl al-kitab who live permanently in *dār al-Islām* according to the conditions of the Pact of Umar.

difaʾ: defense.

faqīh (pl. *fuqāha*): jurists. See *ʿulamā*.

farḍ (pl. *furūḍ*): duty, religious obligation.

farḍ al-ʿayn: individual or personal duty, a duty that must be carried out by the individual without regard to the actions of the community.

farḍ al-kiffāya: a collective duty—a duty that the community has to discharge. The member of the community is considered as having fulfilled it by virtue of his membership in the community.

al-farīḍa al-ghayba: the disappeared duty—title of a book by the Egyptian Islamist Abd al-Salam Faraj. The disappeared duty is the duty of *jihād*.

fatwā (pl. *fatawa*): opinion or ruling by a legal scholar.

fay: war booty.

fasād: corruption—also fasad ʿala al-ard—corruption on earth. Those who cause this state are *mufsidun*.

fiqh: Islamic jurisprudence. See *faqih*.

fitnah (pl. *fitān*): dissent, turmoil.

ghanīma: war booty.

ghazū: war sorties or raids in the early days of Islam.

ghulū: excess.

ḥadīth: a story of the Prophet related by the companions.

haj: the pilgrimage to Mecca—a duty *(farḍ)* for each Muslim once in his lifetime.

ḥalāl: permitted. One of the categories of deeds in Islam. Equated to *jaʾiz*.

ḥarām: forbidden.

ḥarb: war (in general).

ḥarbi: see *kāfir ḥarbi*.

hijra: the migration of the Muslims from Mecca to Medina. Also, in general, migration from a place dominated by heresy to a place ruled by Islam.

hirābah: destruction—see also *muharib*.

Hudaibiyya: a place that symbolizes the classic cease-fire treaty that Muslims are permitted to make.

hudnah (muhādanah): cease-fire or armistice.

ijtihād: independent exegesis of law from direct reading of the sources.

Ikhwān Muslimūn: Muslim Brothers.

Imām: the leader of the community, in Shiite Islam also one of the infallible descendants of Ali.

ijmā': consensus.

istid'af: weakness, in the context of *'ahd al-istid'af*—the period of weakness that obliges Muslims to refrain from provoking the enemy or making temporary cease-fires.

istiftā': a question posed to a Mufti.

istiḥlāl: permitting that which Allah has forbidden. A grave sin sometimes seen as tantamount to apostasy.

istishhād: martyrdom.

istiṣlāḥ: deciding interest—a method of legal reasoning based on taking the interest of the public *(Maslahah)* into account.

ja'iz: permitted. One of the categories of deeds in Islam.

jihād: sanctioned war.

jihād al-difa': defensive *jihād*.

jihād al-nafs: the fight against one's evil inclination.

jihād al-talab wa al-ibtida': *jihād* on the initiative of Muslims for spreading Islam among the infidels.

jihād bi-lisān: *jihād* of the tongue. Usually equated with *da'wah*.

jihād bil-nafs: *jihād* with the soul—sacrifice of oneself in *jihād*.

jihād bi-mal: *jihād* of money. Various forms of supporting *jihād* financially.

jihād fi sabīl allāh: *jihād* for the sake of (in the way of) Allah—physical military *jihād*.

kabīra (pl. *kabāir*): cardinal sin, according to some, may make a Muslim into an infidel.

kāfir (pl. *kuffār*): infidel, non-Muslim.

kāfir ḥarbi: an infidel from a country at war with Muslims *(dār al-ḥarb)*.

kufr: heresy, infidelity.

Khalīfa: Caliph. Successor to the Prophet as Head of the Ummah.

Khariji (pl. *khawarij*): a sect of early Muslims that, among other tenets, considered waging *jihād* as a cardinal duty.

kitābi: see *ahl al-kitāb*.

Mahdī: the Messiah—(in Shiite Islam, the hidden Imam who returns in the end of days).

ma'aṣum: immune—a person who may not be killed. Also infallible (in Shiite Islam).

madhhab: a school of jurisprudence—(in Sunni Islam—*Hanbali, Shafi'i, Maleki,* and *Hanafi*).

makrūh: reprehensible—one of the categories of deeds in Islam.

mandūb: recommended—one of the categories of deeds in Islamic law.

Marja' taqlīd: source of emulation—(in Shiite Islam, a contemporary mujtahid whose rulings and behavior must be obeyed by his followers [*muqaliddun*]).

mu'ahid (pl. *mu'ahdinun*): those who have a treaty with Muslims.

mu'amallah bi-al-mithl: responding in kind, retaliation. See *Qissas*.

muḍallal: misguided.

mujāhid (pl. *mujāhidūn*): a *jihād* fighter.

mujtāhid: a scholar who performs *ijtihād*. See *ijtihād*.

mu'tazila: the school of Islamic philosophy that emphasizes rationality.

mufsidūn: corrupters, people who cause corruption on earth.

muḥāribūn: destroyers—people who cause *hirabah*.

mulhid: atheist.

mu'min: believer.

munāfiq: hypocrite.

munkar: sinful things that must be avoided.

Muraqib: supervisor—a leader in the Muslim Brotherhood.

Murshid (Murshid 'ām): guide or general guide—the chief leader in the Egyptian Muslim Brotherhood.

murtadd: apostate—a Muslim who has rejected his faith, committed a cardinal sin that makes him an apostate, or converted to another religion. A *murtadd* may be a born Muslim *(murtadd fitri)* or a Muslim who had converted from another religion and relapsed *(murtadd milli)*.

mushrik (pl. *mushrikūn*): polytheists—see *shirk*.

must'amin: a *kāfir* who has an *aman* (writ of safe passage in *dār al-Islām*).

mustaḥabb: recommended. One of the categories of deeds in Islam.

mustakbir: arrogant.

al-nafīr/al-'ām/al-istinfār al-'ām: the general call (to arms)—the situation that ensues in the case of a defensive *jihād*.

naskh: abrogation—a technique of reading the Qur'an according to which later verses abrogate earlier ones. The abrogating verse is then *Nasikh* and the abrogated one is *mansukh*.

nafs ma'aṣūma: a person who may not be harmed.

Niya: intention.

qiṣaṣ: retaliation—"eye for an eye."

qiyas: analogy—a technique of interpreting Islamic law.

Qur'an: the holy book.

Ramaḍan: the month of fasting.

Rasuul: prophet, emissary.

ribāṭ: defense of the borders of *dār al-Islam*.

riddah: apostasy, also *irtidād*. See *murtadd*.

Shahāddah: the declaration of faith ("There is no God but Allah and Muhammad is the Prophet of Allah").

shahīd: martyr.

shar'iah: Islamic law.

sirāt al-mustaqīm: the right path.

siyār: law of nations.

ṣulḥ: peace, reconciliation.

sunna: traditions of the Prophet as legally binding on all Muslims.

shirk: polytheism—association of other gods with Allah or belief in a number of gods.

taghūt: despotism, oppression.

tahrīf: corruption of the Qur'anic text or any sacred text.

takfīr: declaring another individual or group of people infidels.

takhsīs: specification—reading a verse according to its specific context.

tawḥīd: the belief in the uniqueness of Allah, as opposed to *shirk*.

'ulamā (sing. *'alem*)—scholars (see *faqih*).

ummah: the Muslim nation.

'urf: traditional law.

al-walā wa-al-barā: loyalty and rejection—the principle that obliges a Muslim to be loyal to the *ummah* and to reject infidels.

walaya: loyalty—(in Shiite Islam to the Imām).

yawm al-qiyāma: day of resurrection.

zakāt: almsgiving, tithe.

Bibliography

Abou El Fadl, Khaled. *And God Knows the Soldiers: The Authoritative and Authoritarian in Islamic Discourse*. New York: University Press of America, 2001.

———. "Islamic Law and Muslim Minorities: The Juristic Discourse on Muslim Minorities from the Second/Eighth to the Eleventh/Seventeenth Centuries." *Islamic Law and Society* 1 (June 1994): 142–187.

———. *Rebellion and Violence in Islamic Law*. Cambridge: Cambridge University Press, 2001.

———. *Speaking in God's Name: Islamic Law, Authority, and Women*. Oxford: Oneworld, 2001.

Abou El Fadl, Kahled, Tariq Ali, Milton Viorst, and John Esposito. *The Place of Tolerance in Islam*. Boston: Beacon Press, 2002.

Abu Qatadah al-Falastini, "Mo'alem al-Taifah al-Mansoura" (The signs of the victorious community). Unpublished paper.

Abu Ruqiayah, "The Islamic Legitimacy of the Martyrdom Operations." *Nida'ul Islam* (Australia), 16 (December 1996–January 1997).

'Ain Sheikh Yosuf bin Saleh, al-, "Dur al-nissā' fī jihād al-ā'adā'" (The role of the women in the jihād against the enemy), *Salsilat al-buhuth wa-aldirasat al-shar'iya* no. 7; *Markaz al-buhuth wa-aldiragat al-shar'iya*, n.d.

Almond, Gabriel A., R. Scott Appleby, and Emmanuel Sivan. *Strong Religion: The Rise of Fundamentalism Around the World*. Chicago: University of Chicago Press, 2003.

Ansari, M.H. *The Islamic Boomerang in Saudi Arabia: The Cost of Delayed Reforms*. New Delhi: ORF Samskriti, 2004.

Ansari, Said a-Din, al-. "Ghazwat New York wa-Washinton" (The raid on New York and Washington). In *Ghazwat 11 Siptimbir* (The raid of 11

September). *Kitab al-Ansar li-mowajahat al-ḥarb al-salabiyya* 1 (September 2002), pp. 5–50.

Atawneh, Muhammad, al-. "Fatwās and Ifta' in Saudi Arabia: A Study of Islamic Thought, 1971–2000." Unpublished doctoral dissertation, Ben-Gurion University of the Negev, 2004.

Azzam, Abdallah. *Al-difa' 'an ard al-muslimin aham furūḍ al-'ayn* (The defense of the lands of the Muslims: the most important of the individual duties). Jeddah: Dar al-Mujtama', 1987.

———. *Fi al-jihād Ādāb wa-āhkām* (On jihād: morals and rules). n.p.: Matbu'at al-jihād, 1987.

———. *I'lān al-jihād* (Declarations of jihād). Peshawar: Maktab Khidmat al-mujāhidin, n.d.

———. *Ilhaq bi-ilqāfilah* (Join the caravan). London: Azzam Publications, 2001.

Bar, Shmuel *The Muslim Brotherhood in Jordan.* Tel Aviv: Dayan Center, 1998.

Bin Humaid, Sheikh Abdullah bin Muhammad. *Jihād in the Qur'an and Sunnah.* Dar-us-Salam. Saudi Arabia: Maktaba, n.d.

Bonney, Richard. *Jihād from Qur'an to Bin Laden.* Hampshire, England: Palgrave-Macmillan, 2004.

Bunt, Gary R. *Islam in the Digital Age: E-Jihād, Online Fatwās and Cyber Islamic Environments.* London: Pluto Press, 2003.

Cook, Michael. *Forbidding Wrong in Islam.* Cambridge: Cambridge University Press, 2003.

Daftary, Farhad. *The Assassin Legends: Myths of the Isma'ilis.* New York: Tauris, 1995.

Dekmejian, R. Hrair. *Islam in Revolution: Fundamentalism in the Arab World.* New York: Syracuse University Press, 1995.

Eliraz, Giora. *Islam in Indonesia: Modernism, Radicalism, and the Middle East Dimension.* Brighton, England: Sussex Academic Press, 2004.

Feldner, Yotam. "Debating the Religious, Political and Moral Legitimacy of Suicide Bombings: The Debate over Religious Legitimacy." *MEMRI Inquiry and Analysis Series* 53 (May 2001), 54 (June 2001), 65 (July 2001).

Firestone, Reuven. *Jihād: The Origins of Holy War in Islam.* New York: Oxford University Press, 1999.

Friedmann, Yohanann. "The Attitude of Jam'iyyat-i 'ulamā'-I Hind to the Indian National Movement and the Establishment of Pakistan." *Asian and African Studies* 7 (1971): 157–180.

———, "The Jam'iyyat-I 'ulamā'-i Hind in the Wake of Partition." *Asian and African Studies* 11 (1976): 181–211.

———. *Tolerance and Coercion in Islam: Interfaith Relations in the Muslim Tradition.* Cambridge: Cambridge University Press, 2003.

Furnish, Timothy. "Beheading in the Name of Islam." *Middle East Quarterly* (Spring 2005).

Gieling, Saskia. *Religion and War in Revolutionary Iran.* London: Tauris, 1999.

Glassé, Cyril. *The Concise Encyclopedia of Islam.* San Francisco: Harper, 1988.

Hallaq, Wael B. *Islamic Legal Theories: An Introduction to Sunni usul al-fiqh.* Cambridge: Cambridge University Press, 1997.

Hughes, Thomas Patrick. *Dictionary of Islam.* New Delhi: Munshiram Manoharlal Publishers, 1885.

Ibn Taymiyyah. *Al-Siyāsa al-shar'iyya fi Islah al-ra'i wa al-ra'iyya* (The shari'ah policy regarding the reform of the ruler and his flock). Beirut: Dar al-Fikr al-Hadith, n.d.

Jackson, Sherman. *On the Boundaries of Theological Tolerance in Islam: Abu Hamid al-Ghazali's Faysal al-Tafriqa.* Oxford: Oxford University Press, 2002.

Jansen, Johannes J.G. "The Early Islamic Movement of the Kharidjites and Modern Moslem Extremism: Similarities and Differences." *Orient* 27 (March 1986).

Johnson, James Turner. *The Holy War Idea in Western and Islamic Traditions.* Philadelphia: Pennsylvania State University Press, 1997.

Kabha, Mustafa, and Haggai Erlich. "Al-Ahbash and Wahabiyya: Interpretations of Islam." Unpublished paper.

Kaptein, Nico J. G. *The Voice of the 'Ulama: Fatwās and Religious Authority in Indonesia.* Institute of South East Asian Studies, Visiting Researchers Series, 2 (2004).

Kelsay, John. *Islam and War: Study in Comparative Ethics.* Louisville, Ky.: Westminster/John Knox Press, 2004.

Khadduri, Majid. *War and Peace in the Law of Islam.* Baltimore: Johns Hopkins Press, 1955.

Kohlberg, Etan. "Medieval Muslim Views on Martyrdom." *Mededelingen der Koninglijk Nederlandse Akademie van Wetenschappen* 60 (1997): 281–307.

Kubeishi, Muhammad 'Ayyash, al-. "Min Fiqh al-Moqawma—Dirasat Tahliliyya: Al-Moqawma wa-al jihād" (Of the law of resistance—analytical studies: the resistance and the jihād). Unpublished paper, 2004.

Landau-Tasseron, Ella. "Jihād," in *Encyclopedia of the Qur'an*, Jane McAuliff, ed. Leiden, England: Brill Academic Publishers, 2003.

Malka, Haim. "Must Innocents Die? The Islamic Debate over Suicide Attacks." *Middle East Quarterly* (Spring 2003).

Martin, Richard C., Mark R. Woodward, and Dwi S. Atmaja. *Defenders of Reason in Islam: Mu'tazilism from Medieval School to Modern Symbol.* Oxford: Oneworld, 2003.

Masud, Muhammad Khalid. "Being Muslim in a Non-Muslim Polity: Three Alternate Models." *Journal of Institute of Muslim Minority Affairs* 10, 1 (1989): 118–128.

Mernissi, Fatema. *Islam and Democracy: Fear of the Modern World.* Cambridge, Ma.: Perseus, 2002.

Mitchell, Richard P. *The Society of the Muslim Brothers.* Oxford: Oxford University Press, 1969.

Moghadam, Assaf. "The Shi'i Perception of Jihād." *AlNakhlah* (Fall 2003).

Na'im, Abdullahi Ahmed an-. *Toward an Islamic Reformation: Civil Liberties, Human Rights, and International Law.* New York: Syracuse University Press, 1990.

Paz, Reuven. "Global Jihād and the Sense of Crisis: al-Qa'idah's Other Front." *Prism Series of Global Jihād* 1, 4 (2003).

———. *Hitabdut ve-Jihād Ba-Islam Ha-Radikali Ha-Falastini: Ha-Pan Ha-Ra'yoni* (Suicide and jihād in radical Islam: the ideological aspect). Tel Aviv: Tel Aviv University, Dayyan Center, 1998.

Peters, Rudolph. *Islam and Colonialism: The Doctrine of Jihād in Modern History.* The Hague: Mouton, 1979.

———. *Jihād in Classical and Modern Islam.* Princeton: Markus Wiener, 1996.

Pruthi, R.K., ed. *Encyclopedia of Jihād.* New Delhi: Anmol Publications, 2004.

Qaradawi, Yousuf. *Al-fatwā bayna al-indibat wa-al-tasayib* (The fatwā between discipline and neglect). Amman: al-maktab al-Islami, 1995.

Qureishi, N.M. *Landmarks of Jihād*. Lahore: Sheikh Muhammad Ashraf, 1971.

Qutb, Sayyid. *Ma'alim fi al-tariq* (Signs on the road). n.p.: Dar al-Shuruq, n.d.

Rosenthal, Franz. "On Suicide in Islam." *Journal of the American Oriental Society* 66 (1946): 239–259.

Safi, Louay M. *Peace and the Limits of War: Transcending Classical Conceptions of Jihād*. Herndon, Va.: International Institute of Islamic Thought, 2001.

Salam, Muhammad ibn Ahmad al-, 39 *wasilah li-khidmat al-jihād wal-musharikah fihi* (39 ways to serve the jihād and to participate in it). n.p.: 1424 (hijri), 2003.

Shams-a-Din, Ayatollah Sheikh Mohammad Mahdī. *Fiqh al-'unf al-Mosalah fi-l-Islam* (The law of armed violence in Islam). Beirut: al-Mowassat al-dawliya lil-dirasat wa-al-nashr, 2001.

Shepard, William E. "Sayyid Qutb's Doctrine of Jahiliyya." *International Journal of Middle East Studies* 35 (November 2003).

Shirazi, Imām Muhammad. *War, Peace and Non-Violence: An Islamic Perspective*. London: Fountain Books, 2001.

Sivan, Emmanuel. *Radical Islam: Medieval Theology and Modern Politics*. New Haven: Yale University Press, 1985.

Weismann, Itzhak. "Modern Sufi Attitudes Towards the West: Four Naqshabandi Cases." Unpublished manuscript.

Periodicals

Al-Ahram Weekly (Egypt)
Al-Hayyat (London)
Nida'ul Islam Magazine (Australia)
Al-Sabil (Jordan)
Al-Sharq al-Awsat (London)
Al-Shihan (Jordan)
Al-Watan (Kuwait)

Internet Sites

www.islamonline.net
www.al-Islam.org
www.almeshkat.net
www.alminbar.com
www.islam.tc/ask-imam
www.sunnah.org
www.cyberfatwā.de
www.fatwā-online.com
www.islam-qa.com
http://jihaadulkuffaarin.jeeran.com (defunct)
www.jihād-online.net (defunct)
www.qaradawi.net

Index